DATE DUE

DEMCO 38-296

Paris

WORLD BIBLIOGRAPHICAL SERIES

General Editors:
Robert G. Neville (Executive Editor)
John J. Horton

Robert A. Myers   Hans H. Wellisch
Ian Wallace   Ralph Lee Woodward, Jr.

John J. Horton is Deputy Librarian of the University of Bradford and was formerly Chairman of its Academic Board of Studies in Social Sciences. He has maintained a longstanding interest in the discipline of area studies and its associated bibliographical problems, with special reference to European Studies. In particular he has published in the field of Icelandic and of Yugoslav studies, including the two relevant volumes in the World Bibliographical Series.

Robert A. Myers is Associate Professor of Anthropology in the Division of Social Sciences and Director of Study Abroad Programs at Alfred University, Alfred, New York. He has studied post-colonial island nations of the Caribbean and has spent two years in Nigeria on a Fulbright Lectureship. His interests include international public health, historical anthropology and developing societies. In addition to *Amerindians of the Lesser Antilles: a bibliography* (1981), *A Resource Guide to Dominica, 1493-1986* (1987) and numerous articles, he has compiled the World Bibliographical Series volumes on *Dominica* (1987), *Nigeria* (1989) and *Ghana* (1991).

Ian Wallace is Professor of German at the University of Bath. A graduate of Oxford in French and German, he also studied in Tübingen, Heidelberg and Lausanne before taking teaching posts at universities in the USA, Scotland and England. He specializes in contemporary German affairs, especially literature and culture, on which he has published numerous articles and books. In 1979 he founded the journal *GDR Monitor*, which he continues to edit under its new title *German Monitor*.

Hans H. Wellisch is Professor emeritus at the College of Library and Information Services, University of Maryland. He was President of the American Society of Indexers and was a member of the International Federation for Documentation. He is the author of numerous articles and several books on indexing and abstracting, and has published *The Conversion of Scripts and Indexing and Abstracting: an International Bibliography*, and *Indexing from A to Z*. He also contributes frequently to *Journal of the American Society for Information Science*, *The Indexer* and other professional journals.

Ralph Lee Woodward, Jr. is Professor of History at Tulane University, New Orleans. He is the author of *Central America, a Nation Divided*, 2nd ed. (1985), as well as several monographs and more than seventy scholarly articles on modern Latin America. He has also compiled volumes in the World Bibliographical Series on *Belize* (1980), *El Salvador* (1988), *Guatemala* (Rev. Ed.) (1992) and *Nicaragua* (Rev. Ed.) (1994). Dr. Woodward edited the Central American section of the *Research Guide to Central America and the Caribbean* (1985) and is currently associate editor of Scribner's *Encyclopedia of Latin American History*.

VOLUME 206

Paris

Frances Chambers

Compiler

CLIO PRESS

OXFORD, ENGLAND · SANTA BARBARA, CALIFORNIA
DENVER, COLORADO

Publication Data

, 1940-
al series; v. 206)
bliography

016.9′4436

ISBN 1–85109–271–4

ABC-CLIO Ltd.,
Old Clarendon Ironworks,
35A Great Clarendon Street,
Oxford OX2 6AT, England.

———

ABC-CLIO Inc.,
130 Cremona Drive,
Santa Barbara,
CA 93117, USA.

Designed by Bernard Crossland.
Typeset by Columns Design Ltd., Reading, England.
Printed and bound in Great Britain by Bookcraft (Bath) Ltd., Midsomer Norton.

THE WORLD BIBLIOGRAPHICAL SERIES

This series, which is principally designed for the English speaker, will eventually cover every country (and some of the world's principal regions and cities), each in a separate volume comprising annotated entries on works dealing with its history, geography, economy and politics; and with its people, their culture, customs, religion and social organization. Attention will also be paid to current living conditions – housing, education, newspapers, clothing, etc. – that are all too often ignored in standard bibliographies; and to those particular aspects relevant to individual countries. Each volume seeks to achieve, by use of careful selectivity and critical assessment of the literature, an expression of the country and an appreciation of its nature and national aspirations, to guide the reader towards an understanding of its importance. The keynote of the series is to provide, in a uniform format, an interpretation of each country that will express its culture, its place in the world, and the qualities and background that make it unique. The views expressed in individual volumes, however, are not necessarily those of the publisher.

VOLUMES IN THE SERIES

Contents

Contents

Introduction

The island in the river Seine which lies not far from the confluence of the Seine, the Marne, and the Oise is conveniently located, and it is not surprising that this spot, the Ile de la Cité, the heart of today's Paris, has been the site of human occupation since prehistoric times. The history of Paris is lengthy and complex, and to summarize it is to touch upon only its high points. But, even from a brief perusal of the story of the city, two aspects of Parisian history stand out: the city's reputation for intellectual and artistic leadership that has marked it since the Middle Ages; and the role of the city as a centre of opposition to whatever government or groups seek to rule France. These two aspects of Paris recur as dark and bright strands weaving through Parisian history, intertwined so as to place the city in the forefront of revolution and war as well as art and literature.

Historic references to the city we know as Paris begin with Caesar's *Gallic Wars*, and the conquest in 52 BC by the Romans of the Celtic tribe known as the Parisii, and of the island on which stood Lutetia, the tribe's principal *oppidium*, a fortified camp probably established several hundred years earlier. The origin of the name Lutetia is unknown, and may have originated in a pre-Celtic language.

With the advent of the Romans, Lutetia became an administrative centre, acquiring the standard accoutrements of a Roman colonial town: an aqueduct, a forum, an arena, temples, villas, and baths, architectural vestiges of which have been excavated in today's metropolis. As the Celtic Gauls blended with their Roman conquerors, a new civilization, the Gallo-Roman, came into being. Christianity was introduced in the middle of the 3rd century by the city's first bishop, the martyred St. Denis, and the Christian architecture that was to play such a prominent role in the cityscape received its first impulse at this time. From the beginning of the 4th century onward the town was known as Paris, and under that name has had a continuous presence as a European urban centre.

The Gallo-Roman civilization of Paris crumbled in the 4th and 5th centuries with the decline of the Roman empire and under the pressure of migrating Germanic tribes. Perhaps the most memorable event of these centuries for Paris was the turning back in 451 AD of an attempted invasion of the city by the Huns, led by Attila, a rescue credited to Saint Genevieve, the city's patron saint.

At the end of the 5th century, Childeric, the leader of the barbarian Franks, attacked Paris and at the beginning of the 6th century, in 508 AD, Clovis, Childeric's son and heir, made it his capital. Clovis, converted to Christianity, was the first of the Merovingian dynasty that ruled from the Ile de la Cité until 751. Notable among the Merovingians was Dagobert (628-638) during whose decade of rule the Fair of St.-Denis was founded. This medieval trading centre established the commercial importance of the city. The most important structure from this era whose remains can still be seen are parts of the Romanesque abbey of St. Germain-des-Prés.

Paris lost its status as a capital when the Carolingian dynasty succeeded the Merovingian. Charlemagne, who became Holy Roman Emperor in 800, moved his Frankish capital from Paris to Aix-La-Chapelle, leaving the city under the rule of the Count of Paris. The subsequent 9th and 10th centuries were lawless and tumultuous, with Viking marauders repeatedly sacking and looting the city. Ultimately, estranged from the Emperor, the Parisians turned to a succession of feudal lords for their defence, with the result that, in 987, the Count of Paris, Hugues Capet, was elected King of France. Once more and henceforth, Paris was the capital of France.

When Hugues Capet became king, his rule extended over little more then Paris and the Ile-de-France region surrounding the city: autonomous feudal lords ruled much of the French territory and the Kings of England claimed vast areas as hereditary possessions. Yet this small territory was the embryo of France, which, in the course of the succeeding centuries, was to be created as a nation largely in terms of the extension of the power of the rulers of Paris.

The Capetians ruled from 987 to 1328, succeeded by the Valois kings whose dynasty lasted until Henri III was assassinated in 1589. Paris underwent tremendous change during these centuries which span the medieval and Renaissance periods in western European history. In the 11th and 12th centuries the Latin Quarter became an intellectual magnet that drew international scholars to Paris, among them Peter Abelard, Thomas Aquinas, Duns Scotus, and William of Ockham. The University of Paris received a papal charter in 1215, and its most famous college, the Sorbonne, was founded in 1253. The city's cathedral, Notre-Dame de Paris, embodying the Gothic architectural

style, was begun in 1163; the Louvre was built during the reign of
Philippe Auguste (1180-1223) as a royal fortress; and the High Gothic
masterpiece, the Sainte-Chapelle, was constructed during the reign of
Saint Louis (1242-48).

During the 14th century, at the close of the Middle Ages, Paris
suffered through plagues, riots, and war. In 1355 Etienne Marcel, a
wealthy bourgeois, led an insurrection to gain a city constitution for
Paris, but failed. The Hundred Years' War that began in 1340 brought
Paris under English rule from 1420 to 1436; it was during this period
(1429) that the city was unsuccessfully besieged by Joan of Arc. The
first poet of Paris, François Villon (1431-63) wrote his ballads at this
time, and the first press in Paris was set up at the Sorbonne in 1470 by
Guillaume Fichet.

At the beginning of the 16th century, François Ier aspired to the
splendour of a Renaissance monarch, most notably in renovating his
Parisian palace, the Louvre, as a luxury residence. Renaissance
humanism was tarnished in France, however, by the ferocity of the
religious wars between Catholic and Huguenot. Catholic Paris was the
scene of one of the most infamous events of the 16th-century split in
Christendom: the event known as the St. Bartholomew's Day Massacre,
when on the evening of 23 August 1572, and in the early hours of 24
August, Huguenot leaders were treacherously assassinated and Catholic
mobs attacked Protestants in the Paris streets. Religious turmoil was a
keynote of Parisian history for the following decades; in 1590 Paris was
besieged by the Protestant Henri of Navarre, who in the end resolved
the religious conflict by accepting the Catholic faith.

Henri IV was the first king of the Bourbon dynasty. He, too, made
improvements in Paris, extending the Louvre and building the Pont
Neuf, but unfortunately his reign was cut short when he was
assassinated on a Paris street, the Rue de la Ferronnerie, in 1610, a
sinister occurrence that foreshadowed future tragic encounters between
the Bourbons and the city. For, as Henri IV's heirs embarked on a
policy of consolidating the central power of the monarchy, opposition
often came from the city: from its arrogant aristocrats, its strong-
minded and stubborn bourgeoisie, or its unruly and unstable popular
classes. In the mid-17th century, Henri IV's grandson, Louis XIV was
forced to flee the city during the rebellions known as the Fronde.
Perhaps the memory of these years imbued this monarch with an
aversion to the city, contributing to his decision to transfer the royal
court to Versailles in 1671.

Whatever precipitated the move, from 1671 to 1789 the political
lines were drawn between Paris and Versailles. The court and the
monarchy were to reside briefly in Paris – in the Tuileries – during the

minority of Louis XIVs great-grandson, Louis XV, under the Regency of Philippe d'Orleans, but this proved an abbreviated episode. In 1722 the king and his court returned to Versailles and the monarchy remained outside of Paris until Louis XVI and his family were brought to Paris in October 1789 as virtual prisoners.

In the 18th century Paris achieved prominence for the intellectual daring of its political thinkers. As the metropolis had once drawn medieval scholars to the Latin Quarter, the city now drew *philosophes* to the cafés of the Palais Royal. In the summer of 1789 economic and political tensions in Paris exploded in mob violence with the storming of the Bastille, and the Revolution was launched. From 1789 to 1799, Paris was the podium of the Revolution from which the most stirring speeches were delivered and the stage upon which the most dramatic events of the time were enacted. In 1792 the guillotine was set up on the Place de la Révolution (now the Place de la Concorde), and for the most part remained there until 1794. During these two years when the Reign of Terror reached its apogee, 1,019 condemned prisoners were executed on the guillotine: the most shocking was the execution of Louis XVI on 21 January 1793.

The various political turns taken by the Revolution ended when Napoleon Bonaparte grasped power. Under Napoleon, France became the political centre of Europe as a new kind of entity: the nation state. European eyes were riveted on Paris as the capital of this new state, and the continent was soon embroiled in conflicts as not only revolutionary ideas but also French armies crossed neighbouring borders.

After Napoleon's defeat at Waterloo, an attempt to restore the Bourbons to the French throne failed. The first years of the 19th century were tumultuous in Paris. Barricades appeared once more in its streets: the July Revolution of 1830 brought the bourgeois Louis-Phillippe to the throne, and the subsequent Revolution of 1848 made France a short-lived Republic. The arrival of Louis-Napoleon, first as President of the Second Republic in 1848, then, after a *coup d'état* in 1851, as Emperor of the Second Empire, Napoloen III, finally brought stability to the nation.

It was during the reign of Napoleon III that Paris assumed the appearance that it wears today. The Emperor appointed Georges-Eugène Haussmann as Prefect of the Seine in 1853 and over the next two decades, the Emperor and the administrator devised and implemented a bold plan to reconstruct Paris. Under Haussmann's direction vast areas of Paris were scooped out to lay down the wide boulevards so typical of the city today, and the Paris Opera, Charles Garnier's extragavant monument to grandiose Second Empire taste, was built.

The Second Empire came to an abrupt end in 1870 with the defeat of the Emperor's army by the Prussians at Sedan. This sparked another remarkable event in Paris: the Siege of Paris by the Prussians and the establishment of the Paris Commune by Parisian workers and Socialists. During 'la semaine sanglante' (the bloody week) from Sunday 21 May 1871, to Sunday 28 May 1871, the workers' insurrection was crushed by the government's army and Paris was retaken in fierce fighting that claimed at least 17,000 victims in the city.

Calm was restored to Paris with the triumph of the bourgeois Third Republic, the city becoming a mecca for the artists and writers of 'Bohemia'. The Impressionists captured the Parisian sunlight in their paintings. The Eiffel Tower, the first piece of modern architecture in Paris, excited a controversy when it was erected for the 1889 World's Fair. In 1900, a second great World's Fair heralded the 'belle epoque', an era that came to an abrupt end when war broke out in August 1914, and Parisians were startled to find themselves bombed from the air and the target of German long-range guns.

With the end of the Great War, a new Paris appeared: the Paris of the expatriates. Ambitious writers and artists flocked to the city; many were Americans – Ernest Hemingway, Scott Fitzgerald, Henry Miller, Gertrude Stein – but there were also numerous personalities from other countries – Diaghilev, Dali, Joyce – who found Paris conducive to creative expression.

The 'années folles' of the 1920s were followed by the uneasy 1930s, during which political turmoil again increased in Paris. But worse days for Paris were yet to come: with the German attack and armistice of May-June 1940, Paris endured four years of a humiliating Nazi occupation, an era redeemed by Resistance fighters and the insurrection of the people of Paris in August 1944, with persons and events most poignantly commemorated in the names of such Paris streets as Rue Pierre-Brossolette, Rue Jean-Moinon, or Rue Danielle-Casanova and also on modest plaques along the Seine.

In the post-war era, the Fourth Republic made way for the Fifth in 1958. A student explosion in Paris in May 1968 brought the barricades back to Parisian streets, but in general the major post-war controversies in the city have been architectural rather than political, revolving around building projects that have drastically altered the Paris cityscape, such as the building of the skyscraper Montparnasse Tower in 1973; the destruction of Les Halles, the Paris markets; the design of the city's first museum of modern art, the Centre Georges Pompidou; and the renovations made to the Louvre, especially the addition of I. M. Pei's unconventional Pyramid.

Introduction

In the 1990s, as Europe moves closer to union, the future of Paris is linked to whatever role France as a whole will assume in the European Union. Contemporary Paris now faces problems common to other urban centres, concerned with unemployment, housing, crime, drugs, and immigration. Those seeking residence in today's Paris are likely to be immigrants and refugees fleeing economic, social and political disasters in other parts of Europe or the world. How Paris integrates these new residents into its cosmopolitan fabric, and what cures the city finds for its urban maladies will, in large part, determine its future.

The bibliography

This bibliography is designed to provide a guide to published materials on Paris: it is a selective compilation of annotated references to essays, periodical articles, and books covering a wide range of subjects, and follows the standard format of the World Bibliographical Series in its categories and in the information provided in its annotations.

This bibliography is aimed at the English-speaking reader; thus, preference has been given to English-language sources. It also somewhat reflects my own areas of interest and expertise, although I have tried to make the coverage as wide as possible. An overwhelming amount of material has been published on Paris: it is hoped that the 430 items listed in this bibliography will aid readers in deepening their knowledge of this fascinating city.

Acknowledgements

I wish to thank all who have helped me in compiling this work, in patricular Julio Rosario and Betty Jenkins, my colleagues in the Reference Division of the City College of New York Library, for their suggestions regarding material to be included in this bibliography. As always, my thanks go to Stephen Chambers, for his unfailingly good-humoured and patient support of this project.

Paris and Its People

General

1   **A place in the world called Paris.**
Edited by Steven Barclay, illlustrated by Miles Hyman, foreword by
Susan Sontag.   San Francisco: Chronicle Books, 1994. 168p.

A book intended for browsers. Barclay has skimmed modern literature to select more
than 170 fictional or non-fictional passages on Paris, organizing them in this volume
into topical chapters with such titles as 'Rain', 'Love and Solace', 'A City to Die For',
etc. The book's list of credits, p. 153-61, can serve the reader as a source list or
bibliography.

2   **The people of Paris.**
Joseph Barry.   Garden City, New York: Doubleday, 1966. 326p.

An American journalist describes his personal fascination with Paris in this unpre-
tentious book. The Parisians that Barry chooses to interview are celebrities of the
early 1960s – among them, Gabrielle Chanel and Jean-Paul Belmondo – who
exemplify the Parisian life of style and sophistication.

3   **Paris: a literary companion.**
Ian Littlewood.   London: John Murray, 1987; New York: F. Watts,
1988. 246p. maps.

This is not a street-by-street guide to Parisian literary landmarks, but rather an
evocation of the city as presented by those who have written about it. Littlewood
considers six Parisian districts in six chapters, quoting liberally from those authors –
mostly French, English, and American – who have written about the places he
mentions. His selections are well chosen to communicate the ambience of Paris, and
readers will find this book an agreeable armchair tour.

4   **Roissy express: a journey through Paris.**
    François Maspero.   London; New York: Verso, 1994. 270p. map.
    Originally published in French (*Les passages du Roissy-Express*; Paris: Seuil, 1990).
    Maspero and photographer Anaik Frantz spent a month exploring and photographing
    the environs of the thirty-eight stations stops made by the RER B-line train as it
    follows its route through the Parisian suburbs from Roissy-Charles de Gaulle Airport
    on the west side of the city to St.-Remy-les-Chevreuse on the east. Maspero's prose
    and Frantz's photographs document the drabness and *ennui* of the Parisian outskirts
    and reveal the depressing social conditions that prevail in the concrete housing
    developments of a Paris that tourists never see.

5   **Paris.**
    Daniel Noin, Paul White.   New York: Bellhaven Press, 1997. 224p.
    (World Cities Series).
    An up-to-date presentation of the Paris of the 1990s – its economy, housing, and
    neighbourhoods – by two urban sociologists. One chapter of the book quotes Parisians
    as they describe their own experience of the city.

6   **Paris.**
    John Russell, foreword by Rosamond Bernier.   New York: Abrams,
    1989, 1983. 350p.
    An art critic reveals the sophistication of Parisian *savoir-vivre* in this oversized book,
    which presents Paris as a city of art and intellect. The volume is splendidly illustrated
    with more than 310 carefully chosen paintings, pastels, drawings, and photographs.

7   **The flâneur.**
    Edited by Keith Tester.   London: Routledge, 1994. 205p.
    The figure of the *flâneur* (stroller) typifies the Parisian. Editor Keith Tester provides
    an introduction to this collection of essays by various scholars examining the literary
    and artistic aspects of *flânerie*. Of particular interest are 'The flâneur on and off the
    streets of Paris', by Priscilla Parkhurst Ferguson, and 'The artist and the flâneur:
    Rodin, Rilke and Gwen John in Paris', by Janet Wolff.

Pictorial works

8   **Atget's Paris.**
    Eugène Atget, introduction by Laure Beaumont-Maillet.   London:
    Thames & Hudson, 1993. 788p.
    In his artistic photographs, Eugène Atget (1856-1927) distilled the essence of Paris in
    the belle époque. This collection brings together 840 examples of Atget's black-and-
    white photographs of the city, categorized by *arrondissement* (district). It was
    published in France as *Atget Paris* (Paris: Hazan, 1992).

9   **Atget's seven albums.**
Eugène Atget, edited by Molly Nesbit.   New Haven, Connecticut: Yale
University Press, 1992. 428p. (Yale Publication in the History of Art).
Between 1909 and 1915, Eugène Atget compiled seven albums of photographs
recording the Paris of that era. These albums are reproduced here for the first time in
their entirety, with Atget's photographs accompanied by a scholarly text.

10   **The work of Atget.**
Eugène Atget, edited by John Szarowski, Maris Morris Hambourg.
New York: Museum of Modern Art, 1981-85. 4 vols. (Springs
Industries Series on the Art of Photography).
Atget's sometimes eerie but incomparable photographic documentation of Paris. The
volumes cover the following periods: volume one, Old France; volume two, The art of
old Paris; volume three, the *ancien régime*; and volume four, Modern times.

11   **Henri Cartier-Bresson: à propos de Paris.** (Henri Cartier-Bresson:
on Paris.)
Henri Cartier-Bresson, with texts by Vera Feyder, André Pieyre de
Mandiargues.   Boston, Massachusetts: Little, Brown; London: Thames
& Hudson, 1994. 167p.
Produces photographs of Paris by Henri Cartier-Bresson, together with English
translations of two essays on the photographer and his work, both originally written
for the catalogue of an exhibition mounted at the Musée Carnavalet in 1984-85, and
published as *Henri Cartier-Bresson: Paris à vue d'oeil* (Henri Cartier-Bresson: Paris
at a glance) (Paris: Seuil, 1994).

12   **Michel Delacroix's Paris.**
Michel Delacroix, text by Richard Howard, foreword by David Rogath,
preface by Michel Delacroix, edited, designed, and produced by
Marshall Lee.   New York: International Archive of Art, 1990. 198p.
Contains reproductions of paintings of pre-Second World War Paris by the French
naïve artist, Michel Delacroix.

13   **Paris.**
Winnie Denker, Jean-Paul Desprat.   New York: Rizzoli, 1992. 223p.
Jean-Paul Desprat's text supplies historical background to accompany the striking
full-page colour photographs by Winnie Denker that constitute this book. Notre-Dame
de Paris, Sacré-Coeur, the Paris Opera, and the Musée d'Orsay are only a few of the
landmarks included. The book was first published in France as *Paris: fêtes et lumières*
(Paris: festivals and lights) (Suresnes, France: Image/Magie, 1991).

14 **Paris; 148 photographs.**
Robert Doisneau, preface by Blaise Cendrars, translated from the
French by Princess Anne Marie Callimachi. New York: Simon &
Schuster, 1956. 1 vol.

Robert Doisneau's black-and-white photographs communicate the mood of postwar
Paris. The 148 photographs gathered together into this book are grouped into the
thematic categories within which Doisneau worked, among them work, leisure, love of
the arts, love of plants, love of animals, 'L'amour', and children. Those interested in
Doisneau's work will also enjoy Peter Hamilton's *Robert Doisneau: a photographer's
life* (New York: Abbeville Press, 1995. 384p.).

15 **Marville: Paris.**
Charles Marville, Marie de Thezy in collaboration with Roxane
Debuisson. Paris: Hazan, 1994. 735p.

Of most interest in this collection of black-and-white architectural photographs are
those taken by Marville in the mid-19th century as part of an official project to record
Paris on the eve of its reconstruction. The book comprises more than 500 photographs,
accompanied by text in French.

16 **The inside-outside book of Paris.**
Roxie Munro. New York: Dutton Children's Books, 1992. 1 vol.
unpaged.

In this work, colourful illustrations are accompanied by a brief text to introduce
children to such Parisian sights as the Eiffel Tower, the Arch of Triumph, and the
Paris Metro.

17 **Le Paris souterrain de Félix Nadar; 1861, des os et des eaux.**
(The underground Paris of Félix Nadar; 1981, bones and water.)
Philippe Neagu, Jean-Jacques Poutlet-Allamagny, Jean Barrou. Paris:
Caisse Nationale de Monuments Historiques et des Sites, 1982. 64p.

The catalogue of an exhibition of the photographs of Parisian underground areas taken
by Félix Nadar in 1861, during the construction of the new sewerage system. For a
discussion of Nadar's subterranean photography see 'Souvenirs' by Shelley Rice (item
no. 337).

18 **Montparnasse: the golden years.**
Bertrand Poirot-Delpech. Paris: Bookking International, 1990. 70p.

Poirot-Delpech has selected photographs of the Montparnasse quartier's streets, cafés,
and celebrities taken by Man Ray, Robert Brassai, Eugène Atget, and André Kertesz
that capture the mood of this extraordinary district in the 1920s and 1930s.

19 **Paris and its environs displayed in a series of picturesque views.**
Augustus Pugin. London: R. Jennings, 1829-31. 2 vols. in 1.

An early compendium of Parisian views, consisting of more than 200 engravings made
under the superintendence of Charles Heath from drawings directed by Pugin. The
plates are accompanied by topographical and historical descriptions of Parisian sites
by L. T. Ventouillac.

20   **A vision of Paris: the photographs of Eugène Atget; the words of Marcel Proust.**
Edited and with an introduction by Arthur D. Trottenberg.   New York: Macmillan, 1980, 1963. 211p.

Two artists whose work epitomizes *fin-de-siècle* Paris are brought together in this book to recreate the Parisian atmosphere of that time. Atget's photographs are drawn from the collection of Berenice Abbott. The book is an English translation of *Paris du temps perdu* (Paris of days gone by) (Lausanne, Switzerland: Edita, 1963).

Paris and its people: an illustrated history.
See item no. 72.

Geography

General

21 **Paris: hasard ou predestination; une géographie de Paris.** (Paris: chance or fate; a geography of Paris.)
Jacqueline Beaujeu-Garnier. Paris: Diffusion Hachette, 1993. 503p. bibliog. (Nouvelle Histoire de Paris).

The most recent presentation of the geography of Paris by the city's leading geographer. Beaujeu-Garnier is also the author of the earlier *Atlas et géographie de Paris et de la région d'Ile-de-France* (Paris: Flammarion, 1977), a comprehensive two-volume geographical presentation of the city and its surrounding region, accompanied by maps.

Maps and atlases

22 **Atlas de Paris et de la region parisienne.** (Atlas of Paris and the Paris region.)
Jacqueline Beaujeu-Garnier, Jean Bastie, preface by Paul Delouvrier.
Paris: Editions Berger/Levrault, 1967. 963p. maps. bibliog.

The most comprehensive current atlas available for Paris and the Paris Metropolitan area, published under the auspices of the Association Universitaire de Recherches Géographiques et Cartographiques. The volume of text is accompanied by a portfolio of maps (57 cm × 69 cm).

23   **Guide général de Paris: répertoire des rues, avec indication de la plus proche station du Métro/General guide to Paris: with repertory of streets and indication of the nearest Metro station.**
Raymond Denaes.   Paris: Editions L'Indispensable, 1993. 1 atlas. 158p., 194p. maps.

By far the most useful vade-mecum for the visitor to Paris, this pocket-sized street atlas contains maps of *arrondissements* on a scale of 1:20,000. It is indexed by streets and keyed to Metro stops. The atlas also includes lists of useful addresses, diagrams of bus routes, a Metro map, and a fold-out map of the entire city. The title which appears on the cover is *Paris par arrondissement* (Paris by district).

24   **Paris up close: district by district, street by street.**
Vivienne Menkes-Ivry, maps by Richard David Creative.
Lincolnwood, Illinois: Passport Books, 1992. Reprinted with revisions, 1994, 1996. 159p. maps.

Provides a bird's-eye view of the architecture of Paris through the fifty isometric maps created from aerial photographs by a group of technical illustrators especially for this book. The volume also includes essential information on Paris and a useful index to persons mentioned in the text. The British edition has the title *Paris: the ultimate street-by-street map and guide* (London: Duncan Petersen, 1992).

25   **Atlas des Parisiens.** (Atlas of Parisians.)
Daniel Noin [et al.].   Paris; New York: Masson, 1984. 1 atlas. maps. bibliog.

This atlas of the Parisian population, designed by the Centre d'Etudes et de Realisations Cartographiques Géographique of the Centre National de la Recherche Scientifique, comprises more than two hundred pages of coloured maps, and is the most recent atlas mapping Parisian social conditions. The volume includes bibliographical references and an index.

26   **Paris, Ile de France, map; Michelin plan.**
Pneu Michelin.   Paris: Office du Tourism et des Congrès de Paris, 1991. 1 map.

A folded map of Paris on a scale of 1:26,000. The 36 cm × 49 cm map is indexed by tourist points of interest and includes a map of the Metro system and information on airport connections.

27   **According to plan – maps of Paris.**
Catherine Reynolds.   *Gourmet*, vol. 50 (July 1990), p. 28ff.

From the 16th-century Plan de Munster to today's Michelin series, a succession of maps have plotted the expansion of Paris. In this article, Reynolds discusses both historical and modern maps of the city, including the city's most famous cartographic representation, the Plan Turgot.

28 **Catalogue des plans de Paris et des cartes de l'Ile de France: de la généralité, de l'élection, de l'archevêche, de la vicomté, de l'université, du grenier à sel et de la Cour des aydes de Paris, conservés à la section des cartes et plans.** (Catalogue of plans of Paris and maps of the Ile de France: on general aspects, elections, the archbishopric, the viscounty, the university, the salt-works, and the Cour des aydes de Paris, kept in the department of maps and plans.) Léon Vallée. Paris: H. Champion, 1908. 576p. Microfilmed, Notre Dame, Indiana: University Libraries, University of Notre Dame, 1995. 1 microfilm reel.

A bibliography of the maps in the collection of the Bibliothèque Nationale that delineate various historic Parisian boundaries. The volume is also available in microfilm format.

The Paris mapguide; the essential guide to La vie parisienne.
See item no. 52.

The atlas of literature.
See item no. 268.

Geology

29 **La Seine; le bassin parisien aux ages antéhistoriques.** (The Seine; the Paris Basin in prehistoric times.)
Eugène Belgrand. Paris: Imprimerie nationale, 1883. 2 vols. (Histoire Générale de Paris: Collection de Documents Publiés sous les Auspices de l'Edilité Parisienne).

A study of the geology and palaeontology of Paris and the Seine River. The second volume of this work comprises an atlas of maps that includes a section of plates entitled 'Catalogue de mollusques terrestres et fluviatiles des environs de Paris à l'époque quaternaire' (Catalogue of terrestrial and water-borne molluscs in the Paris region during the Quaternary period) by Jules-René Bourguignat.

30 **Paris et environs; les roches, l'eau et les hommes.** (Paris and environs; rocks, water and people.)
Philippe Diffre, Charles Pomerol, with the collaboration of A. Blanc [et al.]. Paris; New York: Masson, 1979. 171p. maps. bibliog. (Guides Géologiques Régionaux).

A field guide to geological excursions in and around Paris. The book includes maps, cross-sections, and field stops for those interested in exploring the geology and hydrology of the Paris area.

31 **Bassin de Paris, Ile de France.** (The Paris Basin, Ile de France.)
Charles Pomerol, Léon-Louis Fergueur.   Paris: Masson & Cie., 1986.
2nd ed. 215p.
A geological guide to the region around Paris.

32 **Geology of France with twelve itineraries and a geological map at
1:2,500,000.**
Charles Pomerol with J. Debelmas [et al.], English translation by
A. Scarth.   Paris: Masson; New York: Masson Pub., USA, 1980. 255p.
maps. bibliog. (Guides Géologiques Régionaux).
The foreword of this translation of *France géologique* (Paris: Masson, 1980) states
that the book is designed as a guide for the serious traveller who desires information
that will allow him 'to look upon a landscape not only with pleasure but with insight'.
After an introduction to the geological history of France, the authors provide twelve
itineraries that travellers can follow, with Paris as the starting point for six of the
twelve. The geology of the Paris Basin, the region in which the city is situated, is
covered on p. 24-53.

Guidebooks

33 **Paris-guide; par les principaux écrivains et artistes de la France.**
(Paris guide; by the leading writers and artists of France.)
Edmond About [et al.], introduction and selection by Corinne Verdet.
Paris: La Decouverte/Maspero, 1983. 243p. (La Decouverte Illustrée).

Comprises selections from one of the most illustrious guidebooks to the city ever
printed, the *Paris guide*, published in two volumes by Librairie Internationale in 1867.
Among those who contributed essays to the work were Eugene Pelletan, 'Histoire de
Paris' (History of Paris); Victor Hugo, 'Paris'; Edmond Fournier, 'Maisons
historiques' (Historic houses); Louis Blanc, 'Le vieux Paris' (Old Paris); Viollet-le-
Duc, 'Les Eglises de Paris' (The churches of Paris); and Félix Nadar, 'Le Dessus et le
dessous de Paris' (Paris above and below ground).

34 **Guide de Paris mystérieux.** (Guide to secret Paris.)
François Caradec, Jean-Robert Masson. Paris: Editions Tchou, 1985.
new ed. 763p. bibliog. (Les Guides Noirs).

Readers who have been intrigued by the elongated angel on the facade of no. 57, Rue
de Turbigo will enjoy perusing this guide to Parisian oddities and enigmas and to the
sites of strange, often sinister events in the city's history. Among the guide's most
useful features are a series of itineraries plotted on Paris that include 'Paris Antique'
(Ancient Paris), 'Les Sept Stations de Saint-Denis' (The seven stations of Saint-
Denis), 'Le Double Paris de Victor Hugo' (The dual Paris of Victor Hugo),
'L'Itinéraire d'une vie: Balzac' (Itinerary of a life: Balzac), 'Le Parisien Claude-
Nicolas Ledoux' (The Parisian Claude-Nicolas Ledoux), 'Sur les Traces de Maldoror'
(Following in the steps of Maldoror), 'Les "Traboules" de Paris', 'À travers la
Semaine Sanglante', 'Fantomas à Paris', 'Retour au Modern Style' (Return to the
modern style), and 'Clefs pour Nadja' (Keys for Nadja).

35 **An architect's Paris.**
Thomas Carlson-Reddig, illustrations by Thomas Carlson-Reddig and
Kelly Carlson-Reddig. London: Pavilion; Boston, Massachusetts:
Little, Brown, and Co., 1993. 166p. map. bibliog. (Pavilion
Architecture/Travel Series).

A personal guide to the architectural highpoints of Paris. The text is enhanced by
graceful line drawings and original water-colours of Parisian buildings.

36 **Kidding around Paris; a family guide to the city.**
Rebecca Clay, illustrated by Mary Lambert. Santa Fe, New Mexico:
J. Muir, 1995. 2nd ed. 61p. maps.

A guide to suitable family recreation in Paris for those travelling with children of eight
years and older. It also includes cultural information selected to appeal to young people.

37 **Les rues de Paris; promenades du marquis de Rochegude à travers
tous les arrondissements de Paris, parcourus de nouveau par
Jean-Paul Clebért.** (The streets of Paris; walks taken by the Marquis
de Rochegude through the districts of Paris, travelled once again by
Jean-Paul Clébert.)
Jean-Paul Clébert. Paris: Club des Librairies de France, 1958. 2 vols.
maps. Reprinted, Paris: Editions Planète, 1966.

Jean-Paul Clébert reconstructs the walks taken in Paris at the turn of the century by
the Marquis de Rochegude, who published them in his *Promenades dans toutes les
rues de Paris par arrondissements: origines des rues, maisons historiques ou
curieuses, anciens et nouveaux hotels, enseignes* (Walks in all the streets of Paris by
district: origin of streets, historic or curious houses, old and new hotels, and signs)
(Paris: Hachette, 1910; new edition, 1921).

38 **Permanent Parisians; an illustrated guide to the cemeteries of Paris.**
Judi Culbertson, Tom Randall. Chelsea, Vermont: Chelsea Green,
1986. 230p. maps. bibliog.

A tour through the city's burial grounds, tombs, and crypts, including: Père Lachaise,
the Panthéon, St. Etienne-du-Mont, Montmartre, St. Vincent, Les Invalides, Passy, St.
Germain-des-Près, the Catacombs, Montparnasse, La Chapelle Expiatoire, St. Denis,
and the suburban cemeteries of Levallois, Batignolles, and Neuilly. Maps of each
cemetery are keyed to a list of its famous dead. The authors provide informative,
anecdotal notes describing the buried and their monuments. The book is illustrated
with photographs.

39 **Undiscovered museums of Paris.**
Eloise Danto. Chicago: Surrey Books, 1991. rev. 2nd ed. 132p. maps.

In keeping with the title of the first edition of this work, *Museums of Paris* (Menlo
Park, California: Eldan Press, 1987), this guide includes information on the renowned
museums of Paris as well as on seventy-five of the lesser-known. Travellers interested
in unusual museum collections should also consult Rachel Kaplan's *Little-known
museums in and around Paris* (New York: H. N. Abrams, 1996. 215p.).

40   **Walking Paris: thirty original walks in and around Paris.**
     Gilles Desmons.   London: New Holland; Lincolnwood, Illinois:
     Passport Books, 1994. 208p. maps.

Desmons emphasizes historic sites in these detailed walking tours, which are
organized by Parisian neighbourhoods.

41   **Cheapskate's guide to Paris; hotels, food, shopping, day trips, and
     more.**
     Connie Emerson.   Secaucus, New Jersey: Carol Publishing Group,
     1996. 197p.

The author of this guide promises to show her readers where to obtain maximum value
in Paris for minimum expense. Two other guidebooks with similiar aims are Sandra A.
Gustafson's *Cheap eats in Paris* (San Francisco: Chronicle Books, 1995. 240p.) and
Cheap sleeps in Paris (San Francisco: Chronicle Books, 1995. 254p.), the former listing
100 bargain restaurants, the latter 100 budget hotels.

42   **A street guide to African Americans in Paris.**
     Michel Fabre, John A. Williams.   Paris: Cercle d'Etudes Afro-
     Americaines; Englewood Cliffs, New Jersey: Du Bois Book Center,
     1996. 206p. (Your Heritage Companion Guide to Paris).

The first guide to trace the African-American presence through the *arrondissements* of
Paris. Fabre and Williams have collected references to approximately 1,500 black
American expatriates who visited or lived in Paris, from writer William Wells Brown
in 1849 to composer Leslie Burrs in 1996. Among those noted are Katharine Dunham,
Charlie Parker, Ralph Ellison, Marcus Garvey, Anna Julia Cooper, Nella Larsen,
Josephine Baker, and Sidney Poitier, to name just a few.

43   **Literary cafes of Paris.**
     Noel Riley Fitch.   Washington, DC: Starrhill Press, 1989. 79p. bibliog.

A charming booklet that locates and describes the Paris coffeehouses where
luminaries of French and expatriate literature gathered. The guide is organized by
neighbourhood. See also Christine Graf's *The cafes of Paris: a guide* (New York:
Interlink Books, 1996. 172p.).

44   **Walks in Hemingway's Paris: a guide to Paris for the literary
     traveler.**
     Noel Riley Fitch.   New York: St. Martin's Press, 1990. 195p.

Fitch provides details of walking tours of sites associated with the Paris sojourn of the
American novelist Ernest Hemingway. Another guide to landmarks associated with
Hemingway's life and his novels is John Leland's *A guide to Hemingway's Paris*
(Chapel Hill, North Carolina: Algonquin Books of Chapel Hill, 1989. 125p.).

45   **Essential Paris.**
     Susan Grossman.   Lincolnwood, Illinois: Passport Books, 1994. 128p.
     maps. (Essential Travel Guide Series).

A handy pocket-sized guide with condensed travel information and photographs.

46 **Walks in Gertrude Stein's Paris.**
Mary Ellen Jordan Haight.   Salt Lake City, Utah: Peregrine Smith,
1988. 143p. maps. bibliog.

The five half-day walking tours described in this book promise the reader an imaginative promenade through time and space. Haight is a capable guide to the Left Bank homes and haunts frequented by Gertrude Stein, her expatriate associates, and her bohemian friends from 1900 to 1940. Haight is also the author of a guide to the Right Bank homes of artists, celebrities, and intellectuals: *Paris portraits, Renoir to Chanel: walks on the Right Bank* (Salt Lake City, Utah: Peregrine Smith Books, 1991. 196p.).

47 **Expatriate Paris; a cultural and literary guide to Paris of the 1920s.**
Arlen J. Hansen.   Berkeley, California: Arcade, 1990. 320p. maps.

This volume documents the homes and haunts of the international group of expatriates who came to Paris in the 1920s to pursue careers in literature, art, and music, among them Ernest Hemingway, William Faulkner, Gertrude Stein, Thomas Wolfe, Henry Miller, James Joyce, Eugene O'Neill, Ford Madox Ford, Robert McAlmon, Sylvia Beach, Adrienne Monnier, Constantin Brancusi, Marc Chagall, Sergei Diaghilev, Igor Stravinsky, Miguel de Unamuno, Luis Bunuel, and Salvador Dali. Hansen has organized his material into thirty-two geographical sections, which can be used for walking tours. The text is cross-referenced by streets, names, and topics.

48 **Knopf guide to the Louvre.**
New York: Knopf, 1995. 395p. maps.

A competent guide to Paris's premier museum. It includes detailed cross-sections and floor plans that facilitate access to the Louvre's magnificent collections and amenities.

49 **Pariswalks.**
Alison Landes, Sonia Landes.   New York: H. Holt, 1991. rev. ed.
272p. maps. (Henry Holt Walks Series).

First published in 1975. The authors of the latest revision of this classic Parisian walking guide lead their readers through five Parisian neighbourhoods: St. Julien le Pauvre, La Huchette, St. Germain des Prés, Mouffetard, and Place des Vosges.

50 **Fodor's 97 Paris.**
Edited by Natasha Lesser.   New York: Fodor's Travel Publications,
1996. 232p. maps. (Fodor's Travel Guides).

The latest edition of the reliable tourist guide that first appeared in 1974 and has been regularly updated since. It includes standard information on accommodation, sightseeing, and dining in Paris, as well as additional information on day trips in the Paris region.

51 **Paris and the Ile de France; a Phaidon art and architecture guide; with over 275 color illustrations and 6 pages of maps.**
Franz H. Mehling, Bernhard Pollmann, Maria Paukert. New York: Prentice-Hall, 1987. 259p.

This work, originally published in German as *Knaurs Kulturfahrer in Farbe: Paris und Ile de* France (Knaur's cultural guide in colour: Paris and the Ile de France) (Munich: Deoemersche Verlagsanstalt Th. Knaur Nachf., 1986), is a copiously illustrated guidebook to the art and architecture of the French capital and the Paris Basin. The part of the book that covers Paris has sections on the city's political and cultural history, churches, cemeteries, secular buildings, districts, streets, squares, parks and gardens, and bridges and fountains. The 'Ile de France' section lists the towns of this *département* alphabetically, from Arcueil to Vincennes, and includes Versailles.

52 **The Paris mapguide; the essential guide to La vie parisienne.**
Michael Middleditch. London; New York: Penguin Book, 1994. 64p. maps.

A convenient pocket atlas-cum-guidebook. It is accompanied by text in six languages (English, French, German, Dutch, Italian, and Spanish) and colourful maps on a scale of 1:10,000 which guide tourists to the sights of Paris.

53 **The best of Paris.**
Christian Millau, Colleen Dunn Bates, Alice Brinton [et al.]. New York: Prentice-Hall, 1990. rev. ed. 442p. maps.

A revised edition of *The best of Paris* (1986) by French food critics Henri Gault and Christian Millau. As well as providing basic travel information, the authors fearlessly apply Millau's discriminating standards in 1,800 reviews of Parisian restaurants, hotels, night clubs, and shops.

54 **Turn right at the fountain: fifty-three walking tours through Europe's most enchanting cities.**
George W. Oakes, with new and additional research material by Alexandra Chapman. New York: H. Holt, 1996. 5th rev. ed. 380p. maps.

Chapter nine of this volume details five walking tours of Paris: a lengthy stroll on the Right Bank (Place de la Concorde to Place des Vosges); two shorter walks on the Left Bank; and two additional rambles – one around the Quartier Invalides and another in Montmartre.

55 **Paris and Versailles.**
Ian Robertson, maps and plans by John Flower. London: Black, 1992. 8th ed. 304p. maps. (Blue Guides).

The latest edition of this well-known guide, which updates the previous edition of 1989. *Paris and Versailles* follows the Blue Guide series format, providing meticulous historical information arranged according to well-planned itineraries.

56   **Architect's guide to Paris.**
Renzo Salvadori, translated from the Italian by Brenda Balich.
Sevenoaks, England: Butterworth Architecture, 1990. 137p. bibliog.
Salvadori leads his readers to 101 Parisian structures of architectural interest.

57   **Guide to revolutionary Paris.**
Jean-Charles Sournia, in collaboration with Benoit Dusart, translated
from the French by Angela Dzelzainis.   Paris: Editions de Sante, 1989.
152p. maps.
A guide to the historic sites connected with events that transpired in Paris during the
Revolution, 1789-99. See also *Les pavés de Paris; guide illustrée de Paris revolution-naire*, by Vicomte Guy de La Batut (Paris: Editions Sociales Internationales, 1937.
2 vols.).

58   **The Time out Paris guide.**
Time Out Magazine, Ltd.   London; New York: Penguin Books, 1995.
4th ed. 346p. maps. bibliog. (A Time Out Guide).
Revised biennially, this guide furnishes more than standard tourist information; for
example, it has sections on longer-term accommodation and study, as well as separate
chapters on Paris for women, for gays and lesbians, and for parents and children.

59   **Paris step-by-step: the definitive guide to the street and sights of
Paris.**
Christopher Turner.   London: Pan Books, 1991; New York:
St. Martin's Press, 1992. 308p. maps.
A true vade-mecum, designed to accompany the visitor on walking tours in Paris.
Turner presents eighteen itineraries, keyed to Metro stops, that can be completed in a
morning or afternoon. Maps of the areas and information on the sights to be seen on
each tour is clearly presented. The book includes details on a short selection of
restaurants.

60   **The food lover's guide to Paris.**
Patricia Wells, photographs by Peter Turnley.   New York: Workman
Pub., 1993; London: Metheun, 1994. 3rd ed. 408p. map.
The updated and expanded third edition of a title first published in 1984, this remains
an informative guide to the city's food. Organized according to types of food
establishment, the book covers all of the places where one can enjoy the best of
Parisian food: restaurants, cafés, tea salons, wine bars, brasseries, *patisseries*, and
boulangeries, as well as stores selling speciality food or beverages, bookstores, and
shops for kitchen- and tableware. Under each heading, the food establishments are
arranged geographically by *quartier*. Wells not only recommends where and what to
eat in Paris, but imparts a fund of information ranging from the history of bread to
how to order in a *charcuterie*. The volume also includes recipes and more than 100
photographs.

61   The guide to the architecture of Paris.

Norval White.   New York: Scribner, 1991. 446p. maps.

A guidebook which also serves as a mini-encyclopaedia of information on Parisian architecture.

Flora and Fauna

62   **Les chats de Paris.** (Cats in Paris.)
  Barnaby Conrad III.   San Francisco: Chronicle Books, 1996. 68p.
A compilation of sixty-two black-and-white photographs with English captions in which feline subjects are captured by the cameras of such 20th-century photographers as Jacques-Henri Lartigue, Edouard Boubat, and Robert Doisneau. Conrad has also compiled a companion volume featuring photographs of Parisian dogs: *Les chiens de Paris* (Dogs in Paris) (San Francisco: Chronicle Books, 1995. 68p.).

63   **Private gardens of Paris.**
  Madison Cox, Marianne McEvoy, photographs by Philippe Perdereau.
  New York: Harmony Books, 1989. 224p.
Through the text and photographs of this book, readers gain entry into some of the most exclusive and beautiful sites in Paris: the city's private gardens, terraces, patios, and courtyards, among them the gardens of Yves Saint-Laurent, Hélène Rochas, James Lord, and Princess Poliakoff.

64   **Guide de la nature: Paris et banlieue.** (Nature guide; Paris and its suburbs.)
  Philippe J. Dubois, Guilhem Lesaffre, drawings by François Desbordes.
  Paris: Editions Parigrammas, 1994. 227p. bibliog.
A guide to the urban ecology of Paris and the Ile de France region.

65   **Paris in bloom.**
  Jean-Pierre Le Dantec, Denise Le Dantec, preface by John Dixon Hunt, photographs by Christopher Baker.   New York: Abbeville Press, 1994. 300p.
The text and splendid full-colour photographs of this book serve as a guide to the renowned parks and public gardens of Paris.

History

General

66 Le Département de la Seine et la Ville de Paris; notions générales et bibliographiques pour en étudier l'histoire. (The Department of the Seine and the City of Paris; general and bibliographical notes to aid historical studies.)
Marius Barroux. Paris: J. Dumoulin, 1910. 442p. bibliog. (Publication du Conseil général de la Seine).
An excellent critical bibliography which evaluates works on the geography, history, historiography, institutions, and topography of Paris.

67 Essai de bibliographie critique des généralités de l'histoire de Paris. (A critical bibliographical essay on the history of Paris.)
Marius Barroux. Paris: H. Champion, 1908. 153p. Reprinted, New York: B. Franklin, 1967. (Burt Franklin Bibliography Reference Series, no. 147).
Although now ninety years old, this bibliography remains indispensable for the study of the history of Paris. Barroux has compiled and annotated more than 800 titles dealing with Parisian history to 1907. The work is completed by Barroux's *Le Département de la Seine et la Ville de Paris* (see item no. 66).

68 Paris.
Hilaire Belloc. London: Metheun, 1929. 6th ed. 431p. maps.
A general survey of Paris from the Roman city of Lutetia to the 18th century. Although outdated in many aspects, Belloc's work is still useful especially in regard to the city in the Middle Ages.

69   **A traveller's history of Paris.**
     Robert Cole.   New York: Interlink Books; Oxford: Windrush Press,
     1994. 309p. maps. bibliog. (A Traveller's History Series).

In this book an American university professor chronicles the history of Paris from the
Roman establishment of an administrative centre, Lutetia Parisiorum, on the islands in
the Seine in 53 BC, to 1992 and the building of the Eurodisney amusement park. The
main part of the book is a chronologically organized, lucid presentation of historical
information about Paris. Added chapters summarize facts on topics such as 'Notre-
Dame Cathedral', 'The Louvre', 'Historic Churches', 'Historic Buildings', 'Monuments
to Modernity', 'Paris Parks', 'Bridges on the Seine', 'Cemeteries', and 'Museums and
Galleries in Paris'.

70   **Paris in the past; from Fouquet to Daumier.**
     Pierre Courthion, translated from the French by James Emmons.
     Lausanne, Switzerland: Skira, 1957. 149p. bibliog. (The Taste of Our
     Time).

The colourplate illustrations of this small but informative handbook present Paris as
depicted in painting from the Middle Ages to the end of the 19th century, revealing
what the author terms 'the collective image of Paris' as it developed through the
centuries from the illuminations of early manuscripts to the productions of the
romantics and realists of the 19th-century. The book is carefully documented and
includes a selected bibliography.

71   **Paris on the Seine.**
     Blake Ehrlich.   New York: Atheneum, 1962. 375p. maps. bibliog.

A profusely illustrated history of Paris written for the general public. Ehrlich, a
journalist and freelance writer, has organized his book around the Seine, 'not only the
symbol of the tourist's Paris, but of the Paris of the Parisians and of all the French'.
Ehrlich takes his reader on an imaginary boat ride that follows the Seine downstream
'through seven miles of cityscape and two thousand years of history', embarking at
the Pont National and docking at the quai de Grenelle. Short chapters inform the
reader of the history of the sights and landmarks seen along the banks.

72   **Paris and its people: an illustrated history.**
     General editor: Robert Laffont.   London: Methuen, 1958. 292p. maps.

The result of intensive research in picture archives, this group work is an attractive
presentation of images of the city over time.

73   **The story of Paris.**
     Thomas Okey, illustrations by Katherine Kimball.   London: J. M.
     Dent; New York: E. P. Dutton, 1925. rev. ed. 457p. map. bibliog.
     (Mediaeval Towns Series, vol. 15). Reprinted, Millwood, New York:
     Kraus Reprint, 1971.

The standard English history of Paris, replete with many interesting details and
anecdotes about the city from the Roman conquest of Gaul to the Third Republic. The
1925 edition is a revised version of the first edition of 1906, entitled *Paris and its
story*, with the addition of a new second part. Part one covers the history of the city,
and part two comprises a guidebook to the metropolis as it existed in 1925.

74 **Histoire de Paris.** (History of Paris.)
Marcel Raval. Paris: Presses Universitaires de France, 1948. 5th ed.
125p. map. (Que sais-je?)

Raval's compact account is often cited as an accessible overview of the history of Paris. Another excellent French source for the history of the city is *Paris, histoire d'une ville* (Paris, history of a city), edited by Jean-Robert Pitte (Paris: Hachette, 1993. 191p.). For a history of modern Paris, see Bernard Marchand's *Paris: histoire d'une ville (XIXe-XXe siècles)* (Paris: history of a city [19th-20th centuries]) (Paris: Editions du Seuil, 1993. 440p.).

75 **Paris, city of enchantment.**
Ernest Raymond. New York: Macmillan, 1961. 222p.

A history-cum-guidebook of Paris written for the general reader. The author's method is to plot the history of Paris – from Attila to the Second World War – on the contemporary [i.e. 1961] city, in effect 'leading' the reader around Paris, pointing out notable sites and narrating the historical events connected with the sites. The book is undocumented. Pleasant drawings by Gordon Randall and black-and-white photographs complement the text.

Earliest times

76 **Paris antique, des origines au troisième siecle.** (Ancient Paris, from its origins to the 3rd century.)
Paul Marie Duval. Paris: Hermann, 1961. 369p. maps.

The standard modern French account of Paris during the Roman Empire. Duval is also the compiler of *Les inscriptions antiques de Paris* (The ancient inscriptions of Paris) (Paris: Imprimerie Nationale, 1960. 2 vols.).

77 **Paris à l'Epoque Gallo-Romaine.** (Paris during the Gallo-Roman period.)
Felix-George de Pachtère. Paris: Imprimerie Nationale, 1912. 192p. bibliog. (Histoire Générale de Paris: Collection de Documents Publiés sous les Auspices de l'Édilité Parisienne).

This study, based on notes and plans compiled between 1844 and 1889 by Theodore Vacquer, remains an indispensable source for the study of Paris's antiquities. Vacquer's notes are now archived in the *Fonds Vacquer* of the Bibliothèque Historique de la Ville de Paris.

78 **The archaeology of early Paris.**
Philippe Velay, Brigitte Fischer, Dominique Morel, Bailey Young.
Archaeology, vol. 38 (Nov.-Dec. 1985), p. 26-32.
An informative article, one of the few to cover the Lutetia of the Parisii and of the
Romans. The authors first provide an account of the history of the archaeological
investigation of Paris, initiated in the mid-19th century as a result of the excavation of
Paris in conjunction with Napoleon III's vast modernization project. It was at this time
that Theodore Vacquer, an engineer by training, became what amounted to the world's
first municipal archaeologist, compiling extensive and meticulous notes on work-site
discoveries, notes which were later used by Felix-George de Pachtère (see item
no. 77). Following this introduction to Parisian archaeology, the authors summarize
the history of Lutetia from pre-Roman times to the Frankish invasions of the 5th
century, discuss Gallic-Roman relations, and describe a series of gold coins struck by
the Parisii.

79 **Archaeology in an urban setting: excavations at Saint-Pierre-de
Montmartre, 1975-1977.**
Bailey K. Young. *Journal of Field Archaeology*, vol. 5, no. 3
(Fall 1978), p. 319-29.
A scholarly article that details excavations undertaken in the Jardin du Calvaire,
adjoining the Church of Saint-Pierre on Montmartre, where archaeologists have
unearthed remains of Roman, Merovingian, and mediaeval sacred sites. Good
illustrations make the article of interest to the non-specialist.

80 **Montmartre: the history of a hill.**
Bailey K. Young. *Archaeology*, vol. 32, no. 6 (Nov./Dec. 1979),
p. 43-52. map. bibliog.
Montmartre, the 'Mount of Martyrs', traditionally identified as the site of the 3rd-
century martyrdom of Saint Denis, is the highest point in Paris. In this article, written
for the general reader, Young links the traditional legends connected with the hill with
its actual history as evinced in archaeological investigations. He also gives an account
of recent excavations and their results. The article is amply illustrated, and a short
narrative bibliography gives recommendations for further reading.

Guide de Paris mystérieux. (Guide to secret Paris.)
See item no. 34.

Middle Ages

81   **Biography of a cathedral; the living story of man's most beautiful creation, with glimpses, through the centuries, of the pageant that led to Notre Dame.**
      Robert Gordon Anderson.   New York; Toronto: Longmans, Green and Co., 1944. 496p.

This is not the story of Notre-Dame de Paris (as one might suppose from the title) but rather a sweeping history of France and Western Europe, centring on the Parisian cathedral as the culmination of religious life, 52 BC to AD 1239. Anderson explains in his 'Proscenium' that he seeks to tell 'one particular story . . . one chronicle of one great cathedral . . . and the story, implicit in it, of the actors who have played in its immortal drama'. His book begins with the Roman conquest of the island in the Seine that was to become the site of Notre-Dame, and follows the history of Paris through succeeding centuries to the construction of the cathedral, highlighting the influence of personalities on the history of Paris.

82   **The city and the cathedral; a reflection of the glory of the Gothic and the Middle Ages at their high tide in the city by the Seine.**
      Robert Gordon Anderson.   New York: Longmans, Green and Co., 1948. 337p.

Termed by its author a 'sister book', rather than a sequel, to his earlier *Biography of a cathedral* (see item no. 81), the chapters of this work represent 'snapshots' of selected years from 1200 AD to the beginning of the 14th century. Anderson adopts fictional techniques to make this popular work a vivid and imaginative narrative of Paris in the late Middle Ages.

83   **On the bridges of mediaeval Paris; a record of early fourteenth-century life.**
      Virginia Wylie Egbert.   Princeton, New Jersey: Princeton University Press, 1974. 96p. bibliog.

The main body of this book consists of black-and-white illustrations of thirty miniatures, 'Scenes on the Bridges of Paris from MS. fr. 2090-2092', illustrating life in mediaeval Paris, that are reproduced from an illuminated manuscript now in the Bibliothèque Nationale. The manuscript, the *Life of Saint Denis*, was presented to Philippe V on his coronation in 1317 by Gilles, Abbot of Saint-Denis. Egbert provides a general introduction to the volume and descriptive text for each miniature.

84   **The margins of society in late medieval Paris.**
      Bronislaw Geremek, translated from the French by Jean Birrell.
      Cambridge, England: Cambridge University Press, 1987. 319p. (Past and Present Publications).

Geremek focuses on the outcasts of urban mediaeval society in this scholarly book on the social conditions of Parisian prostitutes and criminals. The work was originally published in Polish as *Ludzie marginesu w sredniowiecznym Paryzu XIV-XV wiek*, and the French edition was published in 1976 as *Les marginaux parisiens aux XIVe et XVe siècles* by Flammarion.

85 **Evocation du vieux Paris; vieux quartiers, vieilles rues, vieilles demeures; historiques vestiges, annales et anecdotes.** (Evocation of old Paris; old districts, old streets, old houses; historic remnants, accounts and anecdotes.)
Jacques Hillairet, illustrated by Roger Borries. Paris: Editions de minuit, 1951-54. 3 vols. maps.

An illustrated history of Paris, describing the city as it was in the Middle Ages and the Renaissance. Volume one covers central Paris, volume two, the *faubourgs* (suburbs) and volume three, the surrounding villages.

86 **Daily living in the twelfth century, based on the observations of Alexander Neckham in London and Paris.**
Urban Tigner Holmes, Jr. Madison, Wisconsin: University of Wisconsin Press, 1952. Reprinted, 1964. 337p. map.

This unusual book provides an account of Paris in the year 1180, using information drawn from a number of mediaeval sources, but based chiefly on Alexander Neckham's *De nominibus utensilium.* Neckham was an Englishman born in 1157 who travelled to Paris in the late 1170s to teach at the university there. Holmes's book is not a translation of Neckham's but incorporates most of its text, providing the reader with a first-hand look at the social and intellectual life of 12th-century Paris.

87 **The goodman of Paris (Le Menagier de Paris); a treatise on moral and domestic economy by a citizen of Paris (1393).**
Translated into English with an introduction and notes by Eileen Power. London: Routledge, 1928. 348p. (Broadway Medieval Library).
Reprinted, Geneva: Slatkine Reprints, 1966. 2 vols.

Power's work is the first translation into English of the mediaeval book on Parisian domestic economy entitled *Le Menagier de Paris, traité de morale et d'économie domestique,* written at the end of the 14th century. The volume's anonymous author was a wealthy older man who compiled the work as a manual of household instruction for his young wife. Readers will find in *The goodman of Paris* a charming picture of the domestic and social life of the 14th-century Parisian bourgeoisie.

88 **Two poets of the medieval city.**
Nancy Freeman Regalado. *Yale French Studies,* vol. 32 (1964), p. 12-21.

A brief discussion of two poets of mediaeval Paris: Rutebeuf, author of the 13th-century *Le Miracle de Theophile,* a 'miracle de Notre-Dame'; and François Villon, the 15th-century poet best known for his 'Ballade des pendus'.

89 **Paris and its people under the English: the Anglo-Burgundian regime 1420-1436.**
Guy Llewelyn Thompson. New York: Oxford University Press; Oxford: Clarendon Press, 1991. 276p. (Oxford Historical Monographs).

During the Hundred Years' War (1339-1453), Paris was occupied for sixteen years by the English and their Burgundian allies. This scholarly history, based on the author's doctoral thesis at the University of Oxford, examines the actual conditions obtaining in Paris at several levels during this period of English rule, analysed against a background of shifting English-French political relations.

16th century

90 **Sidelights.**
Lady Charlotte Julia Blennerhassett, translated from the German by Edith Gulcher. New York: Scribner, 1913. 245p. Reprinted, Freeport, New York: Books For Libraries Press, 1968. (Essay Index Reprint Series).
Chapter one of this book, 'The Siege of Paris, 1590', describes Henri IV's investment, or besieging, of Paris in the summer of 1590. With all communications with the provinces cut, the citizens of Paris endured a dreadful famine from May until the siege was lifted at the end of August. The book was originally published in German as *Streiflichter* (Berlin: Gebruder Paetel, 1911. 259p.).

91 **Paris on the eve of Saint Bartholomew: taxation, privilege, and social geography.**
Robert Descimon. In: *Cities and social change in early modern France.* Edited by Philip Benedict. London: Unwin, 1986, p. 69-104.
An essay describing social conditions in Paris in 1571, the year before the Saint Bartholomew's Day Massacre of 24 August 1572.

92 **Beneath the cross: Catholics and Huguenots in sixteenth-century Paris.**
Barbara B. Diefendorf. New York: Oxford University Press, 1991. 272p. maps.
Diefendorf discusses the clash of tolerance and fanaticism in Paris in the late 16th century in this scholarly study of Paris during the Wars of Religion.

93 **Paris city councillors in the sixteenth century; the politics of patrimony.**
Barbara B. Diefendorf. Princeton, New Jersey: Princeton University Press, 1983. 351p. bibliog.
Drawing on archival sources, Diefendorf has constructed a collective biography of the ninety municipal administrators who served at the Hotel de Ville from 1535 to 1575. The volume is a solid contribution to social history.

94 **The massacre of Saint Bartholemew.**
    Henri Nogueres, translated from the French by Claire Elaine Engle.
    New York: Macmillan, 1962. 168p.
A readable account of the dramatic and bloody events that marked Saint Bartholomew's Day, 24 August 1572, in Paris when Catholics, instigated by Catherine de
Médicis and her son Charles IX, attacked and murdered Huguenots. The book was first
published in France as *La Saint-Barthelemy, 24 août 1572* (Paris: R. Laffont, 1959).

17th century

95 **The Paris of Henri IV: architecture and urbanism.**
    Hilary Ballon.   New York: Architectural History Foundation;
    Cambridge, Massachusetts: MIT Press, 1991. 378p. maps.
A study of the link between politics and public architecture in Paris, 1605-10, at the
end of the reign of Henri IV (assassinated in 1610). Henri IV's policy behind the
development of Paris as an urban centre is explored in relation to the building projects
undertaken during his rule: the extension of the Louvre; the completion of the Pont-
Neuf; and the construction of the Place Dauphine, the Place Royale, and the Place de
France. Ballon's successful combination of architectural and political history and his
use of newly-discovered documents make this an essential book for those studying
Renaissance Paris.

96 **The emerging city: Paris in the age of Louis XIV.**
    Leon Bernard.   Durham, North Carolina: Duke University Press, 1970.
    326p. maps. bibliog.
A scholarly study of urban planning in the 17th century and, in particular, of how the
first 'modernization' of Paris was carried out by Louis XIV and his ministers,
especially Jean-Baptiste Colbert. Such urban concerns as transport, pollution, security,
education, and aesthetics are dealt with in the volume.

97 **Les notaires au Chatelet de Paris sous le règne de Louis XIV; étude
    institutionnelle et sociale.** (Notaries at the Chatelet de Paris during the
    reign of Louis XIV; an institutional and social study.)
    Marie-Françoise Limon, preface by Bernard Barbiche.   Toulouse,
    France: Presses universitaires de Mirail, 1992. 463p. map. (Histoire
    Notariale).
A biographical study of the members of the compagnie du Chatelet, the Parisian
notarial corps, set against the background of the Parisian bourgeoisie of which the
notaries were prominent and prosperous members.

98   **Edo and Paris: urban life and the state in the early modern era.**
      Edited by James L. McClain, John M. Merriman, Ugawa Kaoru.
      Ithaca, New York: Cornell University Press, 1994. 483p. maps.
An unusual work consisting of papers presented at a symposium entitled 'Edo and Paris', held at Tokyo Geihinkan in June 1996. In August 1590, the first Tokugawa, Tokugawa Ieyasu (military leader responsible for the unification of Japan) took over the little fishing village of Edo; at almost the same time, the first Bourbon, Henri IV, entered Paris. During the next century, the dynasties founded by these men developed their cities so that by 1700 Edo, today's Tokyo, was the world's most populous metropolis, and Paris was a major European centre. The conference presenters contrast and compare how the Tokugawa shoguns in Edo and the Bourbon kings in Paris managed the tasks of consolidating their rule and renovating and expanding their capitals.

99   **The birth of intimacy: privacy and domestic life in early modern Paris.**
      Annik Pardaihle-Galabrun, translated by Jocelyn Phelps.   Philadelphia: University of Pennsylvania Press, 1991. 241p. bibliog.
An interesting study of how innovations in interior decoration and house furnishings contributed to the changes in social life in Parisian households in the 17th and 18th centuries. The book was published in France as *La naissance de l'intime; foyers parisiens XVIIe-XVIIIe siècles* (Paris: Presses Universitaires de France, 1988. 523p.).

100   **The Fronde; a French revolution, 1648-1652.**
       Orest Ranum.   New York: W. W. Norton, 1995. 386p. maps. bibliog.
A clear explication of two crisis periods in 17th-century Parisian history when the central government was challenged, first in 1649 by dissatisfied magistrates in the Paris *Parlement* and secondly between 1649 and 1652 by rebellious aristocrats. Ranum is especially deft in handling the way in which the people of Paris responded to these events. For an earlier account of Paris as a *frondeur* centre in the first Fronde, see A. Lloyd Moote's *Revolt of the judges: the Parlement of Paris and the Fronde, 1643-1652* (Princeton, New Jersey: Princeton University Press, 1971. 407p.).

101   **Paris in the age of absolutism; an essay.**
       Orest A. Ranum.   New York: Wiley, 1968. 316p. map. bibliog.
       (New Dimensions in History: Historical Cities).
A history and discussion of the transformation of Paris that began in 1600, as it changed from a mediaeval town to an early modern city, set against the political background of the 17th century. Focusing on the political problems of the absolutist court versus the unruly city, Ranum covers the early conflict between Henri III and the Duke of Guise; the resolution of the monarchical crisis by Henri IV; the reign of Henri IV; Louis XIII and Richelieu; the regency of Mazarin and Anne of Austria; the Fronde; and the final consolidation of absolutism by Louis XIV.

102   **City on the Seine: Paris in the time of Richelieu and Louis XIV.**
       Andrew P. Trout.   New York: St. Martin's Press, 1996. 275p.
A study that examines Cardinal Richelieu's and Louis XIV's contributions to Parisian urban renewal and to improvements in river transport during the 17th century.

18th century

103 Law, magistracy and crime in Old Regime Paris, 1735-1789.
Richard Mowery Andrews. New York: Cambridge University Press,
1994. 2 vols.

Andrews has written the history of the two great criminal courts of pre-Revolutionary
Paris, the Chatelet and Parlement, explaining the system of justice in force at the end
of the *ancien régime*, and examining the courts' procedures, judicial doctrines, and
practices.

**104 Fragile lives: violence, power and solidarity in eighteenth-century
Paris.**
Arlette Farge, translated from the French by Carol Shelton.
Cambridge, Massachusetts: Harvard University Press, 1993. 314p.
bibliog.

This book first appeared in France as *La vie fragile* (Paris: Hachette, 1986). From her
careful perusal of the judicial archives of 18th-century Paris and other manuscript
sources, Farge depicts in rich detail the everyday life of the urban working class in
pre-Revolutionary Paris.

**105 Vanishing children of Paris; rumor and politics before the French
Revolution.**
Arlette Farge, Jacques Revel, translated from the French by Claudia
Mieville.   Cambridge, Massachusetts: Harvard University Press,
1991. 146p. map.

A short account, centring around a relatively unknown incident in Parisian history: the
popular revolt that shook the city in May 1750, when the people of Paris rioted,
convinced that the police (backed by the authorities) were engaged in abducting their
children. This book seeks to pin down and interpret what its author calls the
'fragmented, elusive story' of the antecedents, outbreak, and repercussions of this
popular uprising. Based on archival sources, this book was first published in France as
Logiques de la foule (Paris: Hachette, 1988).

106 Formation of the Parisian bourgeoisie, 1690-1830.
David Garrioch.   Cambridge, Massachusetts: Harvard University
Press, 1996. 364p. maps. (Harvard Historical Studies, no. 122).

A work based on thorough research in primary materials. Garrioch states in his
introduction that his book 'is an attempt to trace, through the study of politics and of
power at the local level, the way that politics, demography, ideology, and economic
change conspired to create, by 1830, a Parisian bourgeoisie – a city-wide political and
social class with common interests and a strong sense of its own identity'. The focus
of the study is the Faubourg Saint Marcel, in particular the parish of Saint Médard.

107 **Neighbourhood and community in Paris, 1740-1790.**
David Garrioch.   New York: Cambridge University Press, 1986.
278p. bibliog. (Cambridge Studies in Early Modern History).

A detailed social history of the world of the ordinary Parisian as expressed in his family life, work, religious experience, and leisure activities. Garrioch plumbed the papers of local police officials to determine and evaluate the economic and social conditions prevalent in the *quartiers* of Paris from the mid-18th century to the last decade of the *ancien régime*.

108 **The anatomy of a scientific institution: the Paris Academy of Sciences, 1666-1803.**
Roger Hahn.   Berkeley, California: University of California Press, 1971. 433p. bibliog.

Hahn traces the development of the Academie des Sciences from its inception to the 18th century.

109 **Farce and fantasy: popular entertainment in eighteenth-century Paris.**
Robert M. Isherwood.   Oxford; New York: Oxford University Press, 1986. 324p. bibliog.

Isherwood's purpose in this book is to answer the central question: 'What kind of satisfaction did the [Parisian] spectators derive from the farces of the fairs and boulevards; the equilibrists and funambulists; the conjurers and charlatans; the dabblers in magic, optical illusion, mechanics and phantasmagoria?' Drawing on contemporary manuscript sources, Isherwood makes a meticulous examination of popular amusements in Paris from 1700 to the late 1780s, investigating the social setting in which popular entertainments took place, and providing many details on the types of diversion available to the Parisian populace.

110 **The bakers of Paris and the bread question, 1700-1775.**
Steven Laurence Kaplan.   Durham, North Carolina: Duke University Press, 1996. 761p.

This massive tome completes the exhaustive study of the bread supply of *ancien régime* Paris begun by Kaplan in his *Provisioning Paris: merchants and millers in the grain and flour trade during the eighteenth century* (see item no. 112). Kaplan's second volume picks up the provisioning process at the point where the earlier volume left off: at the Parisian *boulangeries* where the flour acquired from the grain merchants was made into bread, then purchased by consumers.

111 **Lean years, fat years: the 'community' granary system and the search for abundance in eighteenth-century Paris.**
Steven L. Kaplan.   *French Historical Studies*, vol. 10, no. 2 (Fall 1977), p. 197-230.

In this article, Kaplan covers attempts by Parisian officials during the *ancien régime* to institute a storage system for grain in the capital in order to counter recurring traumatic periods of grain scarcity. Officials hoped to utilize an abundance organization consisting of 'every religious, hospital, public assistance, and educational community in the capital which was supposed to hold at the disposal of the authorities a stock of grain'. The major part of Kaplan's article describes the operation of this reserve system.

112 **Provisioning Paris: merchants and millers in the grain and flour trade during the eighteenth century.**
Steven Laurence Kaplan. Ithaca, New York: Cornell University Press, 1984. 666p. bibliog.

As the author of this book states, in *ancien régime* Paris, 'Daily life turned on the need to procure bread'. Bread was not only the dietary mainstay of the Parisian; it was also the supply of grain that drove the economy of pre-Revolutionary France. Kaplan's weighty volume 'focuses on the institution and the action of the provisioning trade for Paris. Its aim is to follow the story of grain from the time the peasant threshed it until the moment that the baker took delivery of it in the form of flour'. The book is well-documented and draws on much unpublished material. The study is continued in Kaplan's *The bakers of Paris and the bread question, 1700-1775* (see item no. 110).

113 **The names of kings: the Parisian laboring poor in the eighteenth century.**
Jeffry Kaplow. New York: Basic Books, 1972. 222p.

In this scholarly study, Kaplow brings a Marxist viewpoint to bear upon the question of 'how and why the Parisian masses were led to take so active a part in the essentially bourgeois French Revolution'. In order to find the wellsprings of political action among the poor, he describes the urban environment, social conditions, attitudes and institutions, patterns of belief, and criminality and beggary as they existed in pre-Revolutionary Paris.

114 **Miracles, convulsions, and ecclesiastical politics in early eighteenth-century Paris.**
B. Robert Kreiser. Princeton, New Jersey: Princeton University Press, 1978. 485p. bibliog.

Kreiser conducted painstaking archival research to compose this careful study of the 'Saint-Médard episode', the so-called miraculous events that took place at the tomb of François de Paris in the Saint-Médard churchyard in Paris. The volume ranges beyond the immediate incident to discuss conflicts within the Catholic Church, the question of Jansenism, and church-state relations at the time.

115 **Le tableau de Paris.** (The picture of Paris.)
Louis-Sebastien Mercier. [n.p.]: A Amsterdam, 1782-88. 12 vols. in 6. Reprinted, Geneva: Slatkine Reprints, 1979.

Through this mammoth, late 18th-century description of Paris and Parisian social life, Mercier constructed and propagated an image of a diverse and multitudinous city that reverberated throughout the 19th century, finding expression in the work of many subsequent authors, in particular that of Victor Hugo. Mercier's *Tableau* has never been translated into English in its entirety but two abridgements exist: *The picture of Paris, before & after the Revolution*, translated with an introduction by Wilfrid and Emilie Jackson (London: G. Routledge & Sons, 1929. 225p.) and *The waiting city; Paris, 1782-88*, translated and edited with a preface and notes by Helen Simpson (Philadelphia: J. B. Lippincott, 1933. 335p.).

116   **Le tableau de Paris.** (The picture of Paris.)
       Louis-Sebastien Mercier, edition directed by Jean-Claude Bonnet.
       Paris: Mercure de France, 1994. 12 vols. in 2. (Librairie de
       Bicentenaire de la Révolution Française).

A meticulous modern edition of Louis-Sebastien Mercier's *Tableau de Paris* (see item
no. 115). The text for the work was established by comparing the edition of 1783-89
with the edition of 1782-88. The editors have included an introduction discussing
Mercier and his work. *Le Tableau de Paris* is also accessible in an abridged French
edition: *Le Tableau de Paris*, introduction and selection by Jeffry Kaplow (Paris: F.
Maspero, 1979. 356p.).

117   **The people of Paris: an essay in popular culture in the 18th
       century.**
       Daniel Roche, translated by Marie Evans in association with Gwynne
       Lewis.   Berkeley, California: University of California Press, 1987.
       277p. (Studies on the History of Society and Culture).

A work of historical cultural anthropology. Roche states that his aim is to disclose an
image of the Parisian popular classes as they developed as an historical entity
'embedded in a larger social environment', and to answer the question of how the
'popular classes of Paris felt and thought in relation to both the modes of production
and social life' in 18th-century pre-Revolutionary Paris. Chapters cover such topics as
housing and consumption, consumer habits, popular dress, reading habits, and life-
styles.

118   **Merchants and luxury markets; the *marchands merciers* of
       eighteenth-century Paris.**
       Carolyn Sargentson.   London: Victoria and Albert Museum in
       association with the J. Paul Getty Museum, 1996. 224p. bibliog.

A scholarly study of the commerce in luxury goods that flourished around the rue St.
Honoré in Paris in the first decades of the 18th century. The trade was in such items as
wigs, fans, and mirrors, and through an examination of merchants' inventories,
archival materials, and other primary records, Sargentson thoroughly annotates this
page in the history of consumption.

119   **Politics and the Parlement of Paris under Louis XV, 1754-1774.**
       Julian Swann.   Cambridge, England; New York: Cambridge
       University Press, 1995. 390p. bibliog.

Swann's book is concerned with the political conflicts between the government under
Louis XV and the Parlement of Paris that began with the Refusal of the Sacraments
crisis in 1754 and ended with the abolition of the Parlement of Paris in 1771. The
crisis of 1754 occurred when members of the Parlement disagreed with the bishops on
the policy of refusing the sacraments to penitents unable to prove that they had
confessed to authorized priests. Louis XV eventually sided with the bishops and exiled
the Parlement members. However, he soon found that he was unable to replace the
Parlement and so reinstated the exiled members later that year, thereby ending the
immediate crisis but not resolving the underlying conflict.

120 **The police of Paris, 1718-1789.**
Alan Williams. Baton Rouge, Louisiana: Louisiana State University
Press, 1979. 328p. maps. bibliog.
The history of the police administration of Paris during the final years of the *ancien
régime*. Williams feels that the study of the 18th-century police is significant because,
as he comments in his preface, 'the creation of the lieutenancy of police in 1667
represents for the French crown – for the French state . . . a decision to reach beyond
its traditional functions of defense and justice to assume, in one city at least, extensive
new responsibilities for public order and public welfare'. An appendix provides brief
biographical data on the fourteen men who served as Lieutenants of Police in Paris.

Revolution, 1789-99

121 **Paris in 1789-94; farewell letters of victims of the guillotine.**
John Goldworth Alger. London: George Allen, 1902. Reprinted, New
York: AMS Press, 1970. 551p. map.
The subtitle of this book is somewhat misleading as only two chapters reproduce
letters from condemned prisoners. Alger's volume is a substantial contribution to the
history of Paris during the Revolution, providing much factual detail. Chapters of
particular interest are those entitled 'The Paris of the Revolution and What Remains of
It [i.e., in 1902]'; 'The Paris Commune'; 'Paris Day by Day: January-June 1794'; and
'Life in Paris'. One of the most useful chapters is that entitled 'The Paris Sections', in
which Alger provides a list of the forty-eight *sections* into which the revolutionary
municipal government redivided Paris in 1790 – information not easily found
elsewhere. In his listing Alger gives the original name of the *section* – usually a
straightforward appellation derived from a principal landmark within its limits – and
then any subsequent names, as the *sections* were renamed to efface religious and
monarchical traces and to keep up with the swinging political pendulum. (For
example, the *section* first called Place Royale was renamed Fédérés and finally
Indivisibilité.) Alger also provides a very useful map of Paris which locates the
sections.

122 **Death in Paris: the records of the Basse-Gêole de la Seine, October
1795-September 1801, Vendemiaire Year IV-Fructidor Year IX.**
Richard Cobb. Oxford; New York: Oxford University Press, 1978.
134p.
In this detailed study of the deaths of 404 persons as recorded in the *Basse-Gêole de la
Seine, procès-verbaux de mort violente (ans III-IX)* (Basse-Gêole de la Seine, reports
of violent deaths [years III-IX]), Cobb pays particular attention to suicides.

123 **Paris and its provinces, 1792-1802.**
Richard Cobb. London; New York: Oxford University Press, 1975.
279p.
A study of relations between the revolutionary régime in Paris and the provinces in the
final decade of the Revolution.

124 **Publishing and cultural politics in revolutionary Paris, 1789-1810.**
Carla Alison Hesse. Berkeley, California: University of California
Press, 1991. 296p. maps. (Studies on the History of Society and
Culture, vol. 12).

Hesse covers both the revolutionary and the Napoleonic periods in this study of the
political aspects of the book trade at a time when politics clashed with newly-
introduced free-market principles. Among the topics discussed are the introduction of
freedom of the press, the demise of the Paris Book Guild, and the effect that
democratization of the publishing industry had on the rights of authors.

125 **Paris in the revolution.**
G. Lenotre [pseud.], translated by H. Noel Williams. New York:
Brentano, 1925. 319p.

Contains concise biographical and historical chapters on revolutionary figures,
organizations, places, and events. Among those covered in the book are Robespierre,
Madame Roland, Charlotte Corday, and Danton.

126 **Women in revolutionary Paris, 1789-1795: selected documents.**
Translated with notes by Darlene Gay Levy, Harriet B. Applewhite,
Mary Durham Johnson. Urbana, Illinois: University of Illinois Press,
1979. 325p. bibliog.

An anthology of approximately seventy-five documents pertaining to women's
concerns that were composed during the French Revolution. The material comprises
petitions, reports, court and police records, etc., each selection translated into English
and prefaced with an introductory paragraph. The compilers provide a general
introduction and a conclusion to the volume, stating in the latter that, 'After June,
1795, it seemed that the women of Paris were a failure as a political force'.

127 **Paris in the Terror: June, 1793-July, 1794.**
Stanley Loomis. Philadelphia, Pennsylvania: Lippincott, 1964. 415p.
bibliog. Reprinted, New York: Richardson & Steirman, 1986.

In this popular account of the Reign of Terror, Loomis vividly narrates the blood-
drenched period of Parisian history, beginning with Charlotte Corday's assassination
of Marat on 13 July 1793 and ending with the execution of Robespierre a year later.

128 **Festivals and the French Revolution.**
Mona Ozouf, translated by Alan Sheridan. Cambridge,
Massachusetts: Harvard University Press, 1988. 378p. bibliog.

Ozouf chooses an interesting perspective to illuminate the ideology of the French
Revolution: her book is a study of attempts at the Revolution to substitute a new civic
religion in France for the country's traditional Christianity. Although the effort failed,
it left behind a complex of classical and republican symbols that remain emblems of
the French nation. The book is a translation of *La fête revolutionnaire, 1789-1799*
(Paris: Gallimard, 1976).

129 **Twelve who ruled: the year of the Terror in the French Revolution.**
R. R. Palmer.   Princeton, New Jersey: Princeton University Press,
1941. 417p. bibliog.

The twelve were Bertrand Barère, Jean-Nicolas Billaud-Varenne, Lazare Carnot, Jean-
Marie Collot d'Herbois, Georges Couthon, Marie-Jean Herault de Sechelles, Robert
Lindet, Prieur de la Côte-d'Or, Prieur de la Marne, Maximilien Robespierre, André
Jeanbon Saint-André and Louis-Antoine Saint-Just – the members of the Committee
of Public Safety who ruled France from September 1793 until the 9th of Thermidor of
the Year II. Still the only scholarly study, this book is considered the definitive
account of the year of the Reign of Terror, which reached its apogee in Paris. An
epilogue traces the survivors after the 9th of Thermidor.

130 **Revolutionary justice in Paris, 1789-1790.**
Barry M. Shapiro.   New York: Cambridge University Press, 1993.
302p.

A well-researched study that focuses on the earlier, Enlightenment-inspired phase of
the Revolution, at the time when the Marquis de Lafayette as leader of the liberal wing
of the Revolution was the key figure. Shapiro centres his study around the
administration of justice during this period, as illustrated by the changing role played
by Lafayette in two celebrated conspiracy cases: the 1789 imprisonment of the Baron
de Besenval, for whose release Lafayette successfully pleaded; and that of the Marquis
de Favras, the first noble to be publicly hanged. The book sheds light on the workings
of the Parisian revolutionary tribunals.

131 **Paris commune.**
Morris Slavin.   In: *Historical dictionary of the French Revolution,
1789-1799.*   Edited by Samuel F. Scott, Barry Rothaus.   Westport,
Connecticut: Greenwood Press, 1985, vol. 2 (L-Z), p. 743-46. bibliog.

A succinct article that provides the facts pertaining to the first Paris Commune, the
radical municipal government that directed Parisian affairs from 1789 to 1795. Slavin
explains the background, establishment, organization, membership, history, and
curtailment of the Paris Commune, which during the initial revolutionary period –
December 1789 to December 1793 – maintained a de facto independence in governing
Paris *vis-à-vis* the central revolutionary government. The Law of 14 Frimaire Year II
(4 December 1793) finally put an end to its power.

132 **Paris in the Revolution: a collection of eye-witness accounts.**
Edited by Reay Tannahill.   London: Folio Society, 1966. 127p.

Tannahill brings together first-hand sources for the study of the Revolution.

133 **The French Revolution in Paris: seen through the collections of the
Carnavalet Museum.**
Jean Tulard, Marie-Helène Parinaud.   Paris: Paris-Musées, 1989.
241p.

The Musée Carnavalet is the historical museum of the city of Paris. In compiling this
volume of illustrations, the authors have selected from the museum's holdings
numerous portraits, documents, and artifacts that graphically display the progress of

the Revolution in Paris. This book was first published in Paris as *La Révolution française à Paris, à travers les collections du Musée Carnevalet* (Paris: Paris-Musée, 1989).

134   **Crime and punishment in revolutionary Paris.**
Antoinette Wills.   Westport, Connecticut: Greenwood Press, 1981.
227p. bibliog. (Contributions in Legal Studies, no. 15).

The *ancien régime* system of justice was completely overturned at the French Revolution and replaced with a new code of criminal justice. In the first half of this book, Wills examines the changes in law and institutions in detail, and in the second half, drawing on criminal court dossiers, indicates how the new administration of justice was reflected in the daily lives of Parisians.

Guide to revolutionary Paris.
See item no. 57.

Consulate and Empire, 1799-1815

135   **Napoleon and Paris: thirty years of history.**
Maurice Guerrini, translated from the French, abridged and edited by
Margery Weiner.   London: Cassell, 1970. 468p. map. bibliog.

A historical narrative written for the general public. Guerrini states in his preface that his aim in his book is 'to reconstruct the great moments shared by the Man and the City. I have traced the stirring events which marked them in chronological order, day by day, and sometimes hour by hour so that the reader may follow Napoleon from his arrival at the Ecole Militaire on 21 October 1784 to his departure from the Elysée on 25 June 1815, a period of thirty years'. Sources for the book include the *Moniteur* (the official gazette of the French government before 1869), contemporary newspapers, and police reports.

136   **Napoleon recaptures Paris, March 20, 1815.**
Claude Manceron, translated from the French by George Unwin.
London: Allen & Unwin, 1968. Reprinted, New York: W. W. Norton, 1969. 307p. map. bibliog.

Napoleon's recapture of Paris in March 1815, led to the Hundred Days, the period between March and June 1815, during which Napoleon reasserted his rule over France before his second abdication and final departure. Manceron's book was originally published in France as *Napoleon reprend Paris* (Paris: Laffont, 1965).

Early 19th century, 1815-70

137 **Medicine at the Paris Hospital, 1794-1848.**
Edwin H. Ackernecht. Baltimore, Maryland: Johns Hopkins
University Press, 1967. 242p.
Ackernecht takes a fresh look at the influence of the physicians at the Faculté de
Médecine de Paris on the field of medicine in the first half of the 19th century, and on
their role in the emergence of 'hospital medicine'.

138 **Imperial masquerade; the Paris of Napoleon III.**
S. C. Burchell. New York: Atheneum, 1971. 370p. map. bibliog.
A broad survey of Parisian social and intellectual life under Emperor Napoleon III,
aimed at the general reader. The state of politics, art, morals, architecture, and opera
are all described, but the author concentrates on literary developments – particularly
the poetry of Baudelaire – as most illustrative of Napoleon III's reign.

139 **Days with the French Romantics in the Paris of 1830.**
Philip Carr. London: Methuen & Co., 1932. 225p.
One of the few books in English to explore the literary and intellectual movement
known as Romanticism as it existed in Paris in the early 19th century. Carr covers the
intellectual and social life of the French writers who belonged to the movement in the
context of the literary salons where they gathered.

140 **Laboring classes and dangerous classes in Paris during the first
half of the nineteenth century.**
Louis Chevalier, translated from the French by Frank Jellinek. New
York: H. Fertig, 1973. 1st American ed. 505p.
First published in 1958 (Paris: Plon), Chevalier's work quickly achieved classic status
for its brilliant analysis of Parisian social history in the early 19th century, as well as
for its author's deft handling of quantitative evidence. Chevalier's central theme is the
inability of Paris to absorb the immigration which doubled the city's population
between 1800 and 1846. The work also contains two absorbing chapters on Balzac.

141 **Disease and civilization: the cholera in Paris, 1832.**
François Delaporte, translated from the French by Arthur Goldhammer,
foreword by Paul Rabinow. Cambridge, Massachusetts: MIT Press,
1986. 256p. bibliog.
An account of the cholera outbreak in Paris in 1832, and the epidemic's social and
economic impact on the metropolis.

142 **Artists and writers in Paris: the Bohemian idea, 1803-1867.**
Malcolm Easton. New York: St. Martin's, 1964. 205p. bibliog.
Easton adopts a sociological perspective in this exploration of the artistic milieu in
which artists and writers collaborated in early 19th-century Paris, covering seven
decades of intense literary-artistic collaboration. The work is based on published
French sources.

143 **Poor and pregnant in Paris; strategies for survival in the nineteenth century.**
Rachel G. Fuchs. New Brunswick, New Jersey: Rutgers University Press, 1992. 325p. maps.
Fuchs follows the social history of impoverished single mothers in 19th-century Paris from 1830 to 1914. Her study combines statistical studies with individual portraits, covering such topics as illegal abortions, child abandonment, and infanticide.

144 **Insurgent identities: class, community, and protest in Paris from 1848 to the Commune.**
Roger V. Gould. Chicago: University of Chicago Press, 1995. 253p. map.
Gould covers protest movements in Paris from the February Revolution of 1848 to the 1871 Commune.

145 **The world of the Paris cafe; sociability among the French working class, 1789-1914.**
W. Scott Haine. Baltimore, Maryland: Johns Hopkins University Press, 1996. 325p. (The Johns Hopkins University Studies in Historical and Political Science, 114th series, no. 2).
A serious study of the place occupied by the café in the lives of 19th-century working men and women in Paris, and how the café as a social institution contributed to the formation of urban life of that time. Drawing on previously untapped sources, Haine opens a new perspective on the role of the café in the history of the Parisian working class, investigating the café in relation to such topics as political activity, prostitution, and gender issues.

146 **Policing prostitution in nineteenth-century Paris.**
Jill Harsin. Princeton, New Jersey: Princeton University Press, 1985. 417p. bibliog.
Harsin draws on archival records to detail the attempts of social hygienists, moral reformers, government officials, and the police to control and regulate the behaviour of Parisian prostitutes and working-class women suspected of prostitution. In so doing, she reveals 19th-century attitudes towards prostitution and the intrusion of state authority into women's lives.

147 **The American in Paris.**
Jules Janin, illustrated with eighteen engravings by Eugene Lami. London: Longman, Brown, Green & Longmans; New York: Appleton & Son, 1843. 256p. (Heath's Picturesque Annual for 1843).
A mid-19th-century French view of the American visitor in the French capital. For a view of Parisian society of the time by an American, see *Parisian sights and French principles, seen through American spectacles* by James Jackson Jarves (New York: Harper & Brothers, 1852. 264p.).

148   **The beast in the boudoir: petkeeping in nineteenth-century Paris.**
      Kathleen Kete.   Berkeley, California: University of California Press,
      1994. 200p.
A serious scholarly study, extensively documented, of the social aspects of owning a
pet in 19th-century Paris. Kete sees the forms of pet-keeping that developed during
this period as a function of tensions within bourgeois society, and she investigates the
inclusion of dogs, cats, and fish as part of the domestic scene to determine what this
activity signified to the middle-class Parisian.

149   **The coachmen of nineteenth-century Paris: service workers and
      class consciousness.**
      Nicholas Papayanis.   Baton Rouge, Louisiana: Louisiana State
      University Press, 1993. 247p.
Papayanis explores an interesting area of labour history on which little has been
written. In this book, he compiles a detailed quantitative profile of the coach drivers
and the owners of Parisian horse-drawn carriages in 19th-century Paris in order to
explore the formation of working-class consciousness among these workers. Among
the subjects he covers are the coachmen's strikes of the time.

150   **Napoleon III and the rebuilding of Paris.**
      David H. Pinkney.   Princeton, New Jersey: Princeton University
      Press, 1958. 245p. maps. bibliog.
The best-known social history of Paris in the era of Napoleon III, Pinkney's book is a
narrative of urban upheaval. His book covers the twenty years of Parisian history
(1850-70) during which Napoleon III and his Prefect of the Seine, Georges
Haussmann, devised and implemented a bold plan to reconstruct Paris. The grand
boulevards of Haussmann remain a symbol of the city; however, a less well-known
aspect of Napoleon III's urban project was the total renovation of the city's water-
supply and sewerage system, designed and engineered by Eugène Belgrand. Pinkney's
book is especially informative on the latter topic.

151   **Paris sewers and sewermen: realities and representations.**
      Donald Reid.   Cambridge, Massachusetts: Harvard University Press,
      1991. 235p.
Reid's book traces the history of waste disposal in Paris from the crude cesspools of
the 18th century to the development of a comprehensive and efficient system of
sewers in the 19th century. The focus of the book is on the history of the sewermen
during this period.

152   **The Bohemians: la vie de Boheme in Paris 1830-1914.**
      Joanna Richardson.   London: Macmillan, 1969. 201p. bibliog.
Richardson states in her 'Introduction' that 'Murger himself, the author of *La Vie de
Boheme*, said that the real Bohemian could exist only in Paris', where one could
pursue a life of 'idleness, frivolity and passionate intensity. . . . a certain way of life
[led] in certain quarters of Paris'. She organizes her book around the meeting places of
the Bohemians, especially the café. Bohemian life in Paris continued throughout the
19th century, 'the great age of Bohemia'. Many minor figures in the movement receive
attention in Richardson's book.

153 **Bohemian Paris: culture, politics, and the boundaries of bourgeois life, 1830-1930.**
Jerrold Seigel.   New York: Viking, 1986. 453p. bibliog.

Seigel uses Henry Murger's *Vie de Boheme* as the point of departure for this insightful treatment of the history of the Parisian Bohemian milieu. According to Seigel, the Bohemian impulse initiated in France by the early 19th-century Romantics extended to the Surrealists of the early 20th century, with such figures as Baudelaire, Rimbaud, Verlaine, Satie, and Apollinaire being central to an understanding of the Bohemian idea. The volume is enhanced by a narrative bibliographical essay, p. 401-04, in which Seigel critiques other historians' accounts of 'Bohemia'.

154 **Paris and the Parisians in 1835.**
Frances Trollope.   New York: Harper, 1836. Reprinted, Gloucester, England: Alan Sutton, 1985. 523p. (Travel Classics).

One of the themes sounded in Mrs Trollope's letters from Paris are changes in the city since the Revolution of 1830. She also delights in recounting her contacts with the Parisian *grand monde* (e.g., her attendance at Madame Récamier's soirées), and describing her visits to such Parisian sights as the Louvre and the Morgue.

155 **Paris: capital of Europe from the Revolution to the Belle Epoque.**
Johannes Willms, translated from the German by Eveline L. Kanes.
New York: Holmes & Meir, 1997. 436p. maps.

At the Revolution and during the Napoleonic era, France took centre stage in political Europe, occupying this position throughout the 19th century. In the forefront of the development of the nation-state, France led Europe in the consolidation of this new version of the state. Willms has written a history of 19th-century Paris as capital of France and thus capital of Europe, a status that was not to be displaced until the First World War.

Siege and Commune, 1870-71

156 **The Siege of Paris.**
Robert Baldick.   New York: Macmillan, 1964. 248p. map. bibliog.

This popular account is not a military history of the Siege of Paris that took place in the autumn and winter of 1870-71, but rather a presentation of life in the French capital during 'the Terrible Year'. The book is organized as a week-by-week narrative of the siege, based on information drawn from the published accounts of those who remained in the besieged city, among whom were Edmond de Goncourt (see item no. 161), Henry Labouchère, and Henry Vizetelly.

157   Paris Babylon; the story of the Paris Commune.
Rupert Christiansen.   New York: Viking, 1995. 435p.

In this wide-ranging popular presentation, Christiansen brackets 1871, the crisis year of the Paris Commune, with events of the years 1869 to 1875. Readers will enjoy Christiansen's revealing anecdotes, but are likely to disagree with some of his quirky interpretations of the events of the time.

158   La Commune di Parigi; saggio bibliografico. (The Paris Commune; a bibliographical essay.)
Giuseppe Del Bo.   Milan, Italy: Feltrinelli, 1957. 142p. (Bibliografie a cura dell'Instituto Giangiacomo Feltrinelli, no. 2).

An inventory of the Feltrinelli collection on the Paris Commune at the Feltrinelli Institute in Milan, this is the most complete bibliography for the history of the 1871 Paris Commune.

159   The communards of Paris, 1871.
Edited by Stewart Edwards, documents translated by Jean McNeil.
Ithaca, New York: Cornell University Press, 1973. 180p. bibliog.

Edwards has assembled the documents found in this book in order 'to illustrate many of the facets of what was an unplanned, unguided, formless revolution. Besides contemporary documents, many of these archival, there are also accounts of participants and observers who later wrote their memoirs'. After an introduction which fills in the background of the origins and history of the Commune, the documents are presented with explanatory prefatory material and footnotes.

160   The Paris Commune, 1871.
Stewart Edwards.   Chicago: Quadrangle Books, 1971. 417p. bibliog.

Based on thoroughgoing archival research, Edwards's history of the Paris Commune is often cited as the most accurate presentation of the events of the time. Useful appendices list major organizations and persons involved in the Commune and give a chronology of events in France from the French Revolution to 1871. Edwards also includes a short narrative bibliographical essay evaluating scholarship on the Commune and locating available documents.

161   Paris under siege, 1870-1871: from the Goncourt journal.
Edmond de Goncourt, edited and translated by George J. Becker, with a historical introduction by Paul H. Beik.   Ithaca, New York: Cornell University Press, 1969. 334p. map.

Reproduces selections from the *Journal des Goncourts* recording the experiences of Edmond de Goncourt during the Siege of Paris. Except for a few irrelevant passages, the complete journal from 20 June 1870, to 20 June 1871 is translated. The editor comments that the recently bereaved Edmond immersed himself for the first and only time in his life in a public happening, roaming everywhere in besieged Paris, and keeping 'a vivid record of what one man felt it was like to live for nearly nine months under the siege, under the brief Prussian occupation, and under the threat of the Commune'. Edmond's sharp powers of observation were used to advantage. In his entry for Tuesday 20 December 1871, he writes: 'Since the siege began the Parisian's walk seems entirely changed. It was a fine way of walking, always a little hurried, but you felt it was leisurely, pleasurable, and aimless. Now everybody walks like a man in a hurry to get home'.

162 **Revolution & reaction; the Paris Commune 1871.**
      Edited by John Hicks, Robert Tucker.   Amherst, Massachusetts:
      University of Massachusetts Press, 1973. 238p. bibliog.

A wide-ranging collection of essays originally published in *The Massachusetts Review*, vol. 12, no. 3 (Summer 1971) to commemorate the centenary of the Paris Commune. Among the essays are Jeffry Kaplow's 'The Paris Commune and the artists', Wallace Fowlie's 'Rimbaud and the Commune', and Royden Harrison's 'Marx, Engels and the British response to the Commune'. The final selection in the volume comprises an English translation of Bertolt Brecht's drama 'The Days of the Commune'.

163 **The fall of Paris, the siege and the Commune, 1870-71.**
      Alistair Horne.   New York: St. Martin's, 1966. 45p. maps. bibliog.
      Reprinted, Baltimore, Maryland: Penguin, 1981.

The author avoids interpretations and provides a lengthy, detailed, and impartial account of the facts pertaining to the Franco-German War, the Siege of Paris, and the Commune. Horne is also the author of a large-sized illustrated history of the Paris Commune, *The terrible year: the Paris Commune, 1871* (London: Macmillan, 1971. 172p.).

164 **Bibliographie de la Commune de 1871 (1871-1970).** (Bibliography
      of the Commune of 1871 [1871-1970].)
      Jean-Leo.   Brussels: Le Grenier du Collectionneur, 1970. 48p.

Compiled as a supplement to Del Bo's bibliography *La Commune di Parigi* (see item no. 158), this work contains an alphabetical list by author of more than 400 books and articles on the Commune not cited by Del Bo, as well as others that appeared in the period 1957-70. Most of the items cited are in French, and some of the entries have brief annotations.

165 **The Paris Commune of 1871.**
      Frank Jellinek.   New York: Oxford University Press, 1937. 447p.
      bibliog.

A study of the Paris Commune that presents events and facts in a Marxist framework.

166 **History of the Commune of 1871.**
      Prosper Lissagaray, translated from the French by Eleanor Marx
      Aveling.   London: Reeves & Turner, 1886. 500p. Reprinted, New
      York: Monthly Review Press, 1967. (Classics of Radical Thought
      Series, no. 7).

Lissagaray was a left-wing journalist during the Paris Commune; his account of the happenings of 1871 is considered to be the best eyewitness account of the event. His volume was translated into English by Karl Marx's daughter.

167   **The Paris Commune: an episode in the history of the socialist movement.**
Edward Mason.   New York: Macmillan, 1930. 386p. Reprinted, New York: H. Fertig, 1968.
An account of the Paris Commune from a liberal viewpoint.

168   **The Paris Commune of 1871; the view from the Left.**
Edited and introduced by Eugene Schulkind, documents translated from the French by Eugene Schulkind, Heather Nicholas.   New York: Grove Press, 1974. 308p. bibliog. (Writings of the Left).
The editor provides a substantial introduction to this collection of documents illustrating the range of thought about the Commune, preceding, during, and after the event. The section of most interest is Section II, 'The Paris Commune as Government: March 18th to May 28th, 1871', which includes newspaper accounts, speeches, resolutions, declarations, decrees, letters, etc. issued by those connected with the Communard régime. A chronology of significant events, p. 19-23, provides a day-by-day account for the crucial year of 1871.

169   **Socialist women during the 1871 Paris Commune.**
Eugene Schulkind.   *Past & Present*, no. 106 (Feb. 1985), p. 124-63.
A scholarly, heavily-documented article that describes the groundbreaking but ultimately fruitless attempts of the Socialist women of Paris to join together in the Union des Femmes pour la Defense de Paris (Women's Union for the Defence of Paris) during the year of the Paris Commune.

170   *Le plissement* and *la flelure*: **the Paris Commune in Vallès's** *L'Insurgé* **and Zola's** *La Débâcle.*
Charles Stivale.   In: *Modernity and Revolution in nineteeenth-century France.*   Edited by Barbara T. Cooper, Mary Donaldson-Evans.   Newark, Delaware: University of Delaware Press; London: Associated University Presses, 1992, p. 143-54.
In this conference paper, Stivale compares how two French novelists, Jules Valles and Emile Zola, presented the Paris Commune in their literary productions.

171   **The war against Paris, 1871.**
Robert Tombs.   New York: Cambridge University Press, 1981. 256p. bibliog.
Tombs illuminates the year of the Paris Commune by viewing it from a unique perspective. His book is a careful study of the French civil war of April-May 1871 in which the Versaillais army crushed the Paris Commune. The focus of the work, based on research in previously untapped records in French archives, is on these government forces.

172 **My adventures in the Commune, Paris, 1871.**
Ernest Alfred Vizetelly.   New York: Duffield & Company, 1914.
368p.

An account of Paris under the Commune, based on personal observation, but written many years after the events described. Vizetelly was the son of Henry Vizetelly, the Paris correspondent for the *Illustrated London News* during the Paris Commune. He states that in his book he has 'aimed rather at giving my readers a general idea of the Commune's successive phases than at penning a complete account of my own varied experiences'. The work is enhanced by twenty-four illustrations.

Art and the French Commune; imagining Paris after war and revolution.
See item no. 320.

Histoire des journaux publiés à Paris pendant le siège et sous la Commune: 4 septembre 1870 au 28 mai 1871. (History of newspapers published in Paris during the Siege and the Commune, 4 September 1870 to 28 May 1871.)
See item no. 415.

Late 19th-early 20th centuries, 1871-1914

173 **Big business and industrial conflict in nineteenth-century France: a social history of the Parisian Gas Company.**
Lenard R. Berlanstein.   Berkeley, California: University of California Press, 1991. 348p.

Berlanstein utilizes empirical data in his scrutiny of the first fifty years of the Compagnie Parisienne de l'Eclairage et du Chauffage par le Gaz (Paris Gas Lighting and Heating Company). He examines the workings of the company from four perspectives: those of the consumers, the managers, the white-collar workers, and the blue-collar labourers. An important contribution of his study is the analysis of the 1899 strike. Berlanstein is also the author of *The working people of Paris, 1871-1914* (Baltimore, Maryland: Johns Hopkins University Press, 1984. 274p.), a broader social history of the Parisian working class in this period.

174 **The adventurous world of Paris, 1900-1914.**
Nigel Gosling.   New York: W. Morrow, 1978. 240p. bibliog.

An attractive evocation of turn-of-the-century Paris, centring on such creative artists as Picasso, Chagall, Satie, and Matisse.

175   **Parisian sketches; letters to the New York *Tribune*, 1875-1876.**
      Henry James, edited with an introduction by Leon Edel and Ilse Dusoir
      Lind.   New York: New York University Press, 1957. 262p.

In this book articles sent by Henry James from Paris as correspondent for the New
York *Tribune* are published together for the first time. James's prose is engrossing as
he writes about Dumas's plays, the Paris theatre, art exhibitions, George Sand, politics
and Paris in the summertime. Although James at this time frequented the literary
salons of Paris, for the most part he excludes references to his private friendships from
his journalism.

176   **Paris 1900; the great World's Fair.**
      Richard D. Mandell.   Toronto: University of Toronto Press, 1967.
      173p. map. bibliog.

A book-length study of the Exposition Universelle Internationale de 1900.

177   **The Bon Marché: bourgeois culture and the department store,
      1869-1920.**
      Michael B. Miller.   Princeton, New Jersey: Princeton University
      Press, 1981. 266p. bibliog.

The history of a Paris landmark, the Bon Marché department store, founded in the late
19th century as a new type of consumer institution by an extraordinary merchant,
Aristide Boucicaut. Miller used original sources to research his account of this
remarkable addition to bourgeois culture. For a broader picture of French consumers
during this period, see Rosalind H. Williams's *Dream worlds, mass consumption in
late nineteenth-century France* (Berkeley, California: University of California Press,
1982. 451p.). Williams draws together material from many sources to describe
consumer life-styles in late 19th- and early 20th-century France.

178   **Paris shopkeepers and the politics of resentment.**
      Philip G. Nord.   Princeton, New Jersey: Princeton University Press,
      1986. 539p. maps. bibliog.

This monograph is a history of the Ligue Syndicale du Travail, de l'Industrie, et du
Commerce (Union League of Labour, Industry and Business), the Parisian shopkeeper
movement, from 1880 to 1914. Nord defines his book as 'a case study, a particular
instance of the larger phenomenon of *petit-bourgeois* protest'. Among the topics
covered are the origins of the Ligue Syndicale in the real decline experienced by small
retailers in Paris in the 1880s; the movement's political migration from left to right in
the 1890s; and the movement's altered political stance from radical reaction to
conservative accommodation in the 1900-14 period.

179   **Paris fin de siècle.**
      Jean Roman, translated by James Emmons.   New York: Arts, Inc.,
      1960. 105p. (Golden Griffen Books/Essential Encyclopedia).

Well-chosen illustrations, some familiar, others new, will delight the reader in this
lavishly illustrated social history of Paris, which covers the period 1880-1914.

180 **The Belle Epoque; Paris in the nineties.**
Raymond Rudorff.   London: Hamilton, 1972. Reprinted, New York:
Saturday Review Press, 1973. 365p. bibliog.

A fast-paced popular presentation, drawn from published sources, of the 1890s, 'a decade of transition and turbulence in Paris'. Rudorff's focus is on society (both high and low), and readers will enjoy his account of the pleasures, amusements, artistic and literary movements, political events, controversies, personalities, and celebrities that engaged the Parisians of the time. For a contemporary account of these years, see *Bohemian Paris of to-day* by William Chambers Morrow from notes and with illustrations by Edouard Cucuel (London: Chatto & Windus, 1899).

181 **Paris and her people under the Third Republic.**
Ernest Alfred Vizetelly.   New York: Frederick A. Stokes Company,
1919; Reprinted, New York: Kraus Reprint, 1971. 316p.

A lively social history of Paris, covering the period 1871-1900. Vizetelly, an Englishman, chronicles Parisian social life – theatres, musical events, etc. – interspersed with accounts of political incidents.

First World War, 1914-18

182 **The Paris gun; the bombardment of Paris by the German long
range guns and the great German offensives of 1918.**
Henry W. Miller.   New York: Jonathan Cape & Harrison Smith, 1930.
288p. maps. bibliog.

Drawing on published and unpublished sources from both the French and the German sides, Miller, an artillery expert, throughly explores the four German offensives against Paris launched in 1918 when the collapse of imperial Russia freed German divisions for a last-ditch effort on the western front. It was during the western campign of 1918 that the German 'super guns' amazed the Allies; in the first attack in March 1918, projectiles from long-range guns situated seventy-four miles from Paris hit the city; three later bombardments occurred in May, June and July before the Germans were routed by the Allies.

183 **Paris bombardé par Zeppelins, Gothas et Berthas.** (Paris
bombarded by Zeppelins, Gothas, and Berthas.)
Maurice Theiry.   Paris: E. de Boccard, 1921. 296p.

During the First World War, the battle reached Paris from the air when the city was bombed by solo German aviators and shelled from long-range by German artillery. This book is one of the few sources to cover these attacks on the city.

184   **Capital cities at war; Paris, London, Berlin, 1914-1919.**
      Edited by Jay Winter, Jean-Louis Robert.   Cambridge, England; New
      York: Cambridge University Press, 1997. 622p. maps. (Studies in the
      Social and Cultural History of Modern Warfare).
The contributors to this collection of essays bring together the findings of their
research to compile what amounts to a social history of Paris (along with London and
Berlin) during the First World War. The essays cover such topics as the impact of
military casualties on the civilian population; wartime changes in the labour market;
industrial mobilization for war; and the effect of the conflict on social relations,
wages, consumption, social policy, housing, urban demography, and public health.

185   **The note-book of an attaché; seven months in the war zone.**
      Eric Fisher Wood, illustrated with fifteen photographs by the author
      and facsimiles of four official documents.   New York: The Century
      Co., 1915. 345p.
Eric Fisher Wood was an architecture student in Paris when war was declared between
France and Germany in August 1914. On 4 August 1914, he offered his services to the
American Embassy, and in his capacity as an attaché saw the beginning of the war in
Paris at firsthand. His book is interesting for its contemporary viewpoint: he details
the panic that seized Paris as the Germans approached the city after the French defeat
at Charleroi; the surprise at the first airplane attacks on the city; and the relief in Paris
when the French army repulsed the German offensive at the Marne.

L'entre deux guerres, 1918-39

186   **Fireworks at dusk: Paris in the thirties.**
      Olivier Bernier.   Boston, Massachusetts: Little, Brown & Company,
      1993. 351p. bibliog.
Bernier writes in his 'Prologue' to this book that between 1930 and 1940 'it had taken
just ten years for the leading country in Europe to become a helpless victim', and he
seeks, in this book, to cover 'the burst of light' in which classic French culture seemed
'to flare brighter than ever, as it it had to give its very best before it disappeared'.
Bernier uses a broad brush to paint a picture of Paris in the 1930s as the world capital
of art, fashion, and chic, and to interpret this world for the English reader. In the
volume he covers some unusual people about whom little has appeared in English.
The work is anecdotal, lightly documented, and based on published French sources.

187   **An American in Paris; profile of an interlude between two wars.**
      Janet Flanner.   New York: Simon & Schuster, 1940. 415p.
This collection of Flanner's short sketches and stories centres around characteristic
Parisian personalities and events. Flanner succeeds in evoking the atmosphere of Paris
in the 1920s and 1930s.

188 **Paris was yesterday, 1925-1939.**
Janet Flanner (Gênet), edited by Irving Drutman. New York: Viking
Press, 1972. 232p.

From 1925 on, Flanner, under her *nom de correspondance* Gênet, regularly reported
on the intellectual and social life of the Parisians in her 'Letter from Paris' column in
the *New Yorker* magazine. *Paris was yesterday* consists largely of articles selected
from this column, as well as from material published in *Vanity Fair*, *Harper's Bazaar*,
and *An American in Paris* (see item no. 187). In her 'Introduction' written for this
collection, Flanner looks back on her life in Paris among the literary expatriates in the
interwar period, in an era when, she comments, 'Paris . . . seemed immutably French'.

189 **The Left Bank revisited: selections from the Paris *Tribune* 1917-1934.**
Edited with an introduction by Hugh Ford, foreword by Matthew
Josephson. University Park, Pennsylvania: Pennsyvania State
University Press, 1972. 334p.

This selection of articles and sketches from the pages of the Paris *Tribune*, 1917-34,
documents what Josephson in his 'Foreword' characterizes as 'the era of the so-called
Lost Generation'. The history of the English-language Paris *Tribune*, the European
edition of the Chicago *Tribune*, is detailed in Hugh Ford's ten-page 'Introduction',
and 'A Paris *Tribune* Who's Who', p. 317-23, identifies the newspaper's contributors.
The selections themselves consist of wide-ranging journalism with all the advantages
and disadvantages of that genre: up-to-the-minute flavour marred by superficiality.

190 **Paris in the twenties.**
Armand Lanoux, translated by E. S. Seldon. New York: Arts, 1960.
106p. (Golden Griffen Books).

An illustrated overview of Paris in the 1920s, in which Lanoux comments on writers,
artists, clothes, morals, and society. The book was first published in France as *Paris
1925* (Paris: Robert Delpire, 1957).

191 **France in ferment.**
Alexander Werth. New York; London: Harper & Bros., 1935. 309p.
maps.

A book reporting on the political unrest in France that led to antiparliamentary riots in
Paris, 6-7 February 1934. The riots were sparked by revelations of official corruption
in the Stavisky Affair, public outrage over which brought about the resignation of the
Radical Socialist government of Camille Chautemps. Royalists sought to exploit the
moment by staging riots in Paris, but the riots were crushed by the new government of
Edouard Daladier.

192 **The crazy years: Paris in the twenties.**
William Wiser. New York: Atheneum; London; Thames & Hudson,
1983. 256p. bibliog.

Wiser highlights the international aspects of the intellectual, artistic, and social life of
Paris in *les années folles*, synthesizing what is known of the life in Paris of such
expatriates as Hemingway, Fitzgerald, Stein, Picasso, Diaghilev, Stravinsky, Joyce,
Beckett, and Dali.

Second World War, 1939-45

193 **The Jews of Paris and the final solution; communal response and internal conflicts, 1940-1944.**
Jacques Adler.   New York: Oxford University Press, 1987. 310p.
bibliog. (Studies in Jewish History).

A scholarly study of the response of organized French Jewry to Nazi barbarism. Adler begins his book with an examination of the national composition of the Jewish population of France, then discusses the contradictory roles played by Jewish organizations as they sought to protect the French Jewish community and, at the same time, act as its representative *vis-à-vis* the Nazis and the Vichy government.

194 **Sur les murs de Paris et de France, 1939-1945.** (On the walls of Paris and of France, 1939-45.)
Pierre Bourget, Charles Lacretelle.   Paris: Hachette Réalités, 1980. 213p.

This book is an enriched edition of its authors' *Sur les murs de Paris, 1940-1944* (On the walls of Paris, 1940-44) (Paris: Hachette, 1959), and shows the Second World War as depicted in German propaganda levelled at the French. The volume consists largely of reproductions of German war posters disseminated in France during the German occupation, with text in French.

195 **Is Paris burning?**
Larry Collins, Dominique LaPierre.   New York: Simon & Schuster, 1965. 376p. Reprinted, Warner Books, 1991. 389p.

Two journalists construct a vivid chronicle of events in Paris as the German occupation collapsed in August 1944. The book is a series of vignettes involving hundreds of characters who participated in the episodes of the time. The title echoes Hitler's question to the Nazi General von Choltitz who prudently defied the Fuhrer's order to destroy the city.

196 **Histoire de la Libération de Paris.** (History of the Liberation of Paris.)
Adrien Dansette.   Paris: A. Fayard, 1946. rev. ed. 531p. maps. bibliog.

The most complete account of the 17 August uprising in Paris, as the Allied armies approached, and of the city's Liberation on 24 August 1944.

197 **Swastika over Paris: the story of the French Jews under Nazi occupation.**
Jeremy Josephs.   Berkeley, California: Arcade, 1989. 256p.

An account of Nazi attempts to carry out plans for the elimination of French Jewry during the German occupation of France in the Second World War. The story of these years in told by two eye witnesses: Armand Kohn, a member of the Rothchild family who remained in Paris under the occupation; and Paulette Szlifke, a young member of the French Resistance, who survived incarceration in a Nazi concentration camp.

198   **The fall of Paris: June 1940.**
Herbert R. Lottman.   New York: Harper Collins Publishers, 1992.
430p. maps. bibliog.
A day-by-day account of events in Paris – both civilian and military, extraordinary
and banal – that took place during the thirty-nine days from Thursday 9 May – when
the Germans pushed through the Netherlands, Belgium, and Luxembourg – to Sunday
23 June 1940, when the armistice was signed. For each day Lottmann lists the sources
– government documents, public accounts, and interviews with participants – from
which he constructed his narrative.

199   **Paris under the occupation.**
Gilles Perrault, Pierre Azema.   New York: Vendome, 1989. 207p.
The reader becomes an eyewitness to the German occupation of Paris, 1940-44,
through the illustrations assembled in this volume by Gilles Perrault, and the
accompanying commentary by Pierre Azema. The book was originally published in
France as *Paris sous l'occupation* (Paris: Belfond, 1987).

200   **Paris in the Third Reich: a history of the German occupation,
1940-1944.**
David Pryce-Jones, picture editor, Michael Rand.   New York: Holt,
Rinehart, & Winston, 1981. 294p.
Pryce-Jones has supplied the text for singular photographs taken by Roger Schall and
André Zucca depicting ordinary French life during the German occupation.

201   **Paris-underground.**
Etta Shiber, in collaboration with Anne Dupré, Paul Dupré, Oscar Ray.
New York: Scribner's, 1943. Reprinted, Garden City, New York:
Garden City Pub. Co., 1944. 392p.; Alexandria, Virginia: Time-Life
Books, 1989.
The personal narrative of an American woman's involvement in the underground
movement in Paris during the German occupation. After aiding British soldiers to
escape occupied France, Shiber was arrested and endured three years' imprisonment
before being exchanged for a German spy.

Postwar period, 1945-

202   **Paris after the liberation, 1944-1949.**
Antony Beevor, Artemis Cooper.   New York: Doubleday, 1994. 479p.
A popular history of the immediate postwar period in the French capital. After a
prelude describing the collapse of France in 1940 and the German occupation, the
authors cover the era that began with the Liberation of Paris in August 1944, and
ended when the Marshall Plan generated France's economic recovery. This period

included the *epuration* (purge) of collaborators, the short-lived De Gaulle republic, the Communist Party's attempts to gain power, and the beginning of the Cold War. Besides scanning many private papers and other unpublished sources for material, the authors have based their book on extensive interviews.

203　**Protest in Paris; anatomy of a revolt.**
　　　Bernard E. Brown.　Morristown, New Jersey: General Learning Press, 1974. 240p. bibliog.

The author was able to observe at firsthand the last phase of the Paris riots in the summer of 1968. His study is both an account of the events of the French uprising that began in Paris in May 1968, and a critical analysis of what he calls the 'meaning of May'.

204　**Paris journal, 1944-1965.**
　　　Janet Flanner, edited by William Shawn.　New York: Atheneum, 1965. 615p.

Janet Flanner was for forty years the *New Yorker* magazine's Paris correspondent, covering political, social, and intellectual life in the French capital. This volume is a selection from her contributions to the magazine.

205　**Paris in the fifties.**
　　　Stanley Karnow.　New York: Times Books/Random House, 1997. 320p.

Karnow, a Pulitzer-Prize-winning journalist, combines his own memories of Paris as a young reporter with day-to-day accounts of what life was like in the existentialist era at the end of the Fourth Republic (1944-58).

206　**France: the events of May-June 1968; a critical bibliography.**
　　　Laurence Wylie, Franklin D. Chu, Mary Terrell.　Pittsburgh, Pennsylvania: Council for European Studies, 1973. 118p.

A bibliography of studies on the Paris riots of 1968.

Biographies, Autobiographies, Memoirs and Diaries

207 **Sebastien Mercier; sa vie, son oeuvre, son temps.** (Sebastien
Mercier; his life, his work, and his times.)
Leon Beclard. Paris: Champion, 1903. 810p. Reprinted, Hildesheim,
West Germany; New York: G. Olms Verlag, 1982.

An important biographical study of Louis-Sebastien Mercier (1740-1814), the son of a
Parisian gunsmith, who became a dramatist and wrote the influential *Tableau de Paris*
(see item nos. 115 and 116).

208 **That summer in Paris: memories of tangled friendships with
Hemingway, Fitzgerald, and some others.**
Morley Callaghan. New York: Coward-McCann, 1963. 255p.
Reprinted, New York; Penguin, 1979.

Callaghan, a Canadian novelist, and his wife, Loretto, spent the summer of 1929 in
Paris. There Callaghan renewed his friendship with Ernest Hemingway, met Scott and
Zelda Fitzgerald, and took part in the literary world of the Left Bank. The climax of
the summer was a boxing match between Hemingway and Callaghan, with Fitzgerald
as timekeeper. Callaghan's reminiscences of this summer, written thirty years later,
provide some startling insights into the psychology of two of 20th-century America's
most influential writers. For a recent commentary on Callaghan's reminiscences, see
the article by Russell Brown, 'Callaghan, Glassco, and the Canadian Lost Generation',
in *Essays on Canadian Writing*, vol. 51-52 (Winter/Spring 1993/94), p. 81-112.

209 **The life and times of Baron Haussmann; Paris in the Second
Empire.**
J. M. Chapman, Brian Chapman. London: Weidenfeld & Nicolson,
1957. 262p. maps. bibliog.

As the authors state, 'It is Paris as Haussmann left her that we know today'. This book
is a compact, straightforward account of Haussmann's public life, based largely on
material drawn from his *Mémoires* (see item no. 213). Born in Paris, Haussmann

entered the prefectural corps and served twenty-three years in provincial posts until Emperor Napoleon III appointed him Prefect of the Seine in 1853. Backed by the Emperor, Haussmann remodelled Paris, both above and below ground: not the least of his achievements was the construction of a new water supply system for Paris. The authors of this book characterize Haussman as 'ebullient, ruthless, and highly intelligent' who, although accused by his critics of bad taste and vandalism, imparted 'a noble, if bourgeois dignity' to Paris, 'a little turgid, somewhat pompous', but still, 'solid and worthy'.

210 The women of Montparnasse.
Morrill Cody, with Hugh Ford.   New York; London: Cornwall Books, 1984. 192p.

Offers Cody's personal reminiscences about the notable women who formed the Left Bank Anglo-American colony in Paris during the interwar years, from the early 1920s to the outbreak of the Second World War. Among those whose lives are described are Sylvia Beach, Gertrude Stein, Lady Duff Twysden, Isadora Duncan, and Nancy Cunard. The book is well illustrated with photographs.

211 An American art student in Paris: the letters of Kenyon Cox, 1877-1882.
Kenyon Cox, edited by Wayne Morgan.   Kent, Ohio: Kent State University Press, 1986. 224p. bibliog.

The correspondence of an American painter provides insight into the Parisian world of the 19th-century art student. Kenyon Cox was a Midwesterner who, after studying in Philadelphia, went to Paris at the age of twenty-one to continue his art studies. The impressions he formed of the Parisian art world from five years spent in the ateliers of painters Carolus-Duran and Gêrome are communicated in his letters. Readers may also be interested in *An art student's reminiscences of Paris in the eighties*, by John Shirley Shirley-Fox (London: Mills and Boon, 1909). Shirley-Fox was an Englishman who in 1882, at the age of fourteen, studied painting at Gêrome's studio in Paris.

212 Four lives in Paris.
Hugh G. Ford, with a foreward by Glenway Westcott.   San Francisco: North Point Press, 1987. 286p.

Ford contemplates four Americans – publisher Margaret Anderson, composer George Antheil, novelist Kay Boyle, and journalist Harold E. Stearns – whose biographies demonstrate the varieties of expatriate intellectual experience in early 20th-century Paris.

213 Mémoires du baron Haussmann. (The memoirs of Baron Haussmann.)
Georges-Eugène, Baron Haussmann.   Paris: Victor-Havard, 1890-93. 3 vols.

The key figure in the mid-19th-century demolition and reconstruction of much of Paris, Haussmann spent 1888 to 1891 – the last three years of his life – compiling these *Mémoires*. The first volume, *Avant l'Hotel de Ville* (Before the City Hall), covers his life before his appointment as Préfet de la Seine; the second and third volumes, *Préfecture de la Seine* (Prefecture of the Seine) and *Grands travaux de Paris* (Public works in Paris), describe his official years and the rebuilding of Paris. These memoirs have served as the basis of most later biographical writing on Haussmann. *Le Paris du Baron Haussmann; Paris sous le second Empire* (The Paris of Baron Haussmann; Paris under the Second Empire), edited by Patrice de Moncan, Christian Mahout (Paris: Seesam RCI, 1991. 415p.), reprints selections from Haussmann's third volume.

214   **A moveable feast.**
Ernest Hemingway.   New York: Scribner, 1964. 211p.
Hemingway's portrayal of his life and literary apprenticeship in Paris in the 1920s has become a literary classic, and remains unmatched in its evocation of the atmosphere of the time. For a recent study of the book that separates fact from fiction in Hemingway's account of his Paris years, see Jacqueline Tavernier-Courbin's *Ernest Hemingway's A Moveable feast: the making of a myth* (Boston, Massachusetts: Northeastern University Press, 1991. 261p.).

215   **Between meals: an appetite for Paris.**
A. J. Liebling, with an introduction by James Salter.   New York: Modern Library, 1995. 182p. (Modern Library).
A. J. Liebling (1904-63) was known for his contributions to the *New Yorker* magazine. This selection of his writings on Paris, first published in 1962, is now reissued in the Modern Library Series with a twenty-three-page introduction by James Salter. Recounting his own experiences, Liebling emphasizes his sensory and, in particular, gastronomic adventures in the city.

216   **Journal of my life.**
Jacques-Louis Ménétra, with an introduction and commentary by Daniel Roche, translated from the French by Arthur Goldhammer, foreword by Robert Darnton.   New York: Columbia University Press, 1986. 368p.
Jacques-Louis Ménétra was a Parisian glazier born in 1738 who wrote this autobiography sometime between 1764 and 1802. In it he describes the life of a working-class man during the *ancien régime*, touching on such topics as sex, marriage, friendship, violence, work, and religion. The book is enhanced by Daniel Roche's lengthy commentary which provides the nonspecialist reader with the historical background to Ménétra's text. The work was published in France as *Journal de ma vie: Jacques-Louis Ménétra, compagnon vitrier au 18e siècle* (Journal of my life: Jacques-Louis Ménétra, master glazier in the 18th century) (Paris: Montalba, 1982), transcribed from a manuscript in the Paris archives.

217   **Grand obsession: Madame Curie and her world.**
Rosalynd Pflaum.   New York: Doubleday, 1989. 496p.
From 1883 to 1905, Marie Curie and her husband Pierre carried out their ground-breaking experimental work at the Ecole de Physique et de Chimie industrielles in the 20th *arrondissment*'s Rue Pierre-Brossolette. Pflaum's biography of the scientist combines a tactful human tale with a technical exposition of Madame Curie's important discoveries, set against a solidly-researched background of the Parisian world of the Curies' milieu.

218 **My life.**
Edith Piaf with Jean Noli, translated from the French and edited by
Margaret Crosland. London: Owen, 1990. 120p.

The ultimate *chanteuse*, whose Paris accent is immortalized in her recordings, Edith
Piaf (1915-63) dictated these reminiscences to Jean Noli shortly before her death. In
this English translation, Piaf exposes her personality and the rigours of her life,
although she says little about her music. For those interested in Piaf, Margaret
Crosland's *Piaf* (New York: Putnam, 1985. 240p.) is considered to be a balanced
summary of the singer's life.

219 **Vidocq, a biography.**
Philip John Stead. New York: Roy Publishers, 1954. 263p.

Eugène-François Vidocq (1775-1857) was at various times a soldier in Napoleon's
army, an army deserter, a petty criminal, and an escaped convict. He was also
instrumental in creating the Paris police, and served as chef de la Sûreté (Head of
Intelligence). His life and adventures are said to have served as the model for Balzac's
extraordinary character Vautrin in the *Comédie humaine*. The author of this biography
of Vidocq has also written *The police of Paris* (London: Staples Press, 1957. 224p.).

220 **The great good place: American expatriate women in Paris.**
William Wiser. New York: Norton, 1991. 336p. bibliog.

A popular treatment of the lives of five American women – Mary Cassatt, Edith
Wharton, Caresse Crosby, Zelda Fitzgerald, and Josephine Baker – who, according to
Wiser, 'passed the most critical or significant years of their lives in France'. A
separate chapter summarizes each woman's life, stressing her Parisian experiences.
Wiser's book is undocumented but readable. Each chapter is prefaced by a full-page
photograph of its subject.

221 **Notable or notorious?: a gallery of Parisians.**
Gordon Wright. Cambridge, Massachusetts: Harvard University
Press, 1991. 147p.

Wright has chosen to research and write chapter-length biographies of 19th-century
Parisians who were well known in their day but are now largely forgotten: Delphine
Gay de Girardin, Eugene Sue, Allan Kardec, Clemence Royer, Juliette Adam, Marquis
de Mores, 'Diana Vaughan' [Leo Taxil], Ernest Constans, Theophile Steinlein, and
Charles Péguy. Readers will appreciate this book for its insight into an ambiguous
world.

**Les notaires au Chatelet de Paris sous le règne de Louis XIV; étude insti-
tutionnelle et sociale.** (Notaries at the Chatelet de Paris during the reign of
Louis XIV; an institutional and social study.)
See item no. 97.

Paris under siege, 1870-1871: from the Goncourt journal.
See item no. 161.

The note-book of an attaché; seven months in the war zone.
See item no. 185.

Kiki's Paris: artists and lovers, 1900-1930.
See item no. 326.

Gustave Eiffel.
See item no. 400.

Population

222   **Behind the bamboo hedge; the impact of homeland politics in the Parisian Vietnamese community.**
Gisele L. Bousquet.   Ann Arbor, Michigan: University of Michigan Press, 1991. 196p. bibliog.

One of the few studies in English on the Vietnamese in Paris. The author states that 'the Vietnamese community in Paris is the oldest and largest one in France, with a population officially estimated at fifty thousand. . . . [the Vietnamese] do not live in a specific area [but are] spread to all areas of the city'. In this study of political ethnicity, Bousquet differentiates the long-established pre-1975 Vietnamese from the newly arrived post-1975 refugees in their involvement with the politics of their ethnic homeland. Chapters cover 'The Role of History in the shaping of a Political Identity'; 'Politics among the Vietnamese Immigrants in Paris'; 'Vietnamese Immigrants and Refugees as an Ethnic minority in France'; 'The Pro-Hanoi Faction'; and 'The Anti-Communist Faction'.

223   **Polish Jews in Paris: the ethnography of memory.**
Jonathan Boyarin.   Bloomington, Indiana: Indiana University Press, 1991. 195p. map. (The Modern Jewish Experience).

A scholarly study of a Parisian immigrant community: the Labor Zionist, Communist, and ex-Communist Yiddish-speaking Jews who survived the Holocaust and immigrated to France. This book is based on fieldwork conducted by the author in 1982-83, during which time he observed the activities of Jewish societies in Paris and interviewed the members of these organizations. From this material, he has constructed a careful ethnographic description of the everyday lives of Parisian Jews of Eastern European origin.

224 **La formation de la population parisienne au XIXe siècle.** (The
formation of the population of Paris in the 19th century.)
Louis Chevalier. Paris: Presses Universitaires de France, 1950. 312p.
maps. bibliog. (Institut National d'Etudes Démographiques. Travaux et
Documents; Cahiers no. 10).

Chevalier's first book is an in-depth analysis of the growth and evolution of the
Parisian population. The first part of the volume discusses the impact of migration
from other regions of France during the first half of the 19th century on the
demography of Paris. The second and third parts analyse how migration affected the
Parisian economic and social milieux. The book is extensively documented from
primary sources, and includes a meticulous bibliography.

225 **The Pletzl of Paris: Jewish immigrant workers in the 'Belle
Epoque'.**
Nancy L. Green. New York: Holmes & Meier, 1986. 270p. bibliog.

During the last decades of the 19th century, East European Jews began arriving in
France in large numbers, many of them to live and work in the Marais district of Paris,
which became known as the Pletzl, or 'little square'. Green's book is a case-study of
these Jewish immigrant workers, and represents an important contribution both to the
history of the French labour movement and to the history of ethnic relations in Paris.

226 **Le triangle de Choisy; un quartier chinois à Paris: cohabitation
pluri-ethnique, territorialisation communautaire et phénomènes
minoritaires dans le 13e arrondissement.**
Michelle Guillon, Isabelle Taboada-Leonetti. Paris:
C.I.E.M.I./L'Harmattan, 1986. 210p. (Migrations et Changements,
no. 7).

A sociological study of the inhabitants of the 'Chinatown' of Paris, located in the
thirteenth *arrondissement* within a quadrilateral bordered by the Rue de Tolbiac on the
north, the Rue Nationale on the east, the Boulevard Masséna to the south, and the Avenue
de Choisy on the west.

227 **The modernization of North African families in the Paris area.**
Andrée Michel. The Hague: Mouton, 1972. 387p. bibliog. (New
Babylon: Studies in the Social Sciences, no. 16).

This sociological study on inter-ethnic relations presents the results of research
conducted in 1966-67 on the 'acculturation of Algerian immigrants in France in
relation to French values and norms relative to the nuclear family'. It considers how
'modern' Algerian workers and their wives have become in their attitudes towards
family size, contraception, and education. Nine hundred and fifty North African men
and women living in the Paris area were interviewed for this study.

228 **The African immigrant population of Paris.**
Tacco Ndongo. In: *Human rights in urban areas.* Paris: UNESCO, 1983, p. 89-101.

A survey of immigrants from Senegal, Mali, and Mauritania who are working as dustmen, Metro cleaners, railway workers, stokers or housewives in Paris. The purpose of the study was to obtain information about the obstacles these Africans encounter in practising their own life-style in Paris. Among the problems noted are insufficient access to education, French-language training, housing, or work. The immigrants also experience difficulties in following African traditional practices with regard to clothes, food, and family relations.

229 **Migrations to Paris during the Second Empire.**
David H. Pinkney. *Journal of Modern History*, vol. 25, no. 1 (March 1953), p. 1-12.

During the 1850s and 1860s a migratory flow from the provinces to Paris contributed to an unusually large population increase in the metropolis. The author of this study has selected for detailed study three *départements* that contributed heavily to this migration – the Creuse, the Haute-Saone, and the Seine-et-Marne. From his research in archival resources, Pinkney concludes that economic motives and increased opportunities in the capital attracted the provincial immigrants.

230 **South-East Asian refugees in Paris: the evolution of a minority community.**
Paul White, Hilary Winchester, Michelle Guillon. *Ethnic and Racial Studies*, vol. 10, no. 1 (January 1987), p. 48-61. map. bibliog.

A study of the Chinese in Paris's 'Chinatown' in the thirteenth *arrondissement*. The authors state that 'the objective of the present contribution to the literature is to examine the impact of a sector of the refugee population in creating a distinctive ethnic concentration within a single European city, and to consider how this area developed in relation to established ideas of the evolution of "Chinatowns"'. From their scrutiny of the Parisian Chinese district existing among high-rise apartment blocks, the authors conclude that the Chinese concentration in Paris is atypical of the 'Chinatowns' that have developed in other urban environments.

Atlas des Parisiens. (Atlas of Parisians.)
See item no. 25.

Language

231 **The migrant languages of Paris.**
L.-J. Calvet. In: *French today; language in its social context.*
Edited by Carol Sanders. Cambridge, England; New York:
Cambridge University Press, 1993, p. 105-19.

Calvet discusses the situation in Paris of the major foreign languages spoken in the French capital by groups migrating from outside France. He notes the absence of a consistent governmental linguistic policy and that 'the only model entertained in France is that of the assimilation by migrants and especially by the children of migrants of French language and culture'. Commenting on Parisian multilingualism, Calvet notes that linguistic interaction among migrant groups is lacking: 'Paris is a good illustration of the co-existence of numerous languages which share the same linguistic and geographic territory without ever meeting'.

232 **Les accents des français.** (The accents of French.)
Fernand Carton [et al.]. Paris: Hachette, 1983. 94p. map. bibliog.
(De Bouche à Oreille).

An explanatory booklet and an audiocassette tape illustrating the pronunciation of French in different areas of France.

233 **La prononciation parisienne; aspects phoniques d'un sociolècte parisien (du faubourg Saint-Germain à La Muette).** (Parisian pronunciation; phonic aspects of a Parisian sociolect [from Saint-Germain to La Muette].)
Odette Mettas. Paris: SELAF, 1979. 564p. bibliog.

A sociolinguistic study of the social aspects of the speech and pronunciation patterns of an area in Paris. The work is in French, but the text is summarized in English, Russian, and Spanish.

Society, Health and Welfare

234 **Trajectories in living space, employment and housing stock:**
the example of the Parisian metropolis in the 1980s and 1990s.
Martine Berger. *International Journal of Urban and Regional*
Research, vol. 20, no. 2 (June 1996), p. 240-54. maps. bibliog.
An article on population distribution, labour supply, and residential mobility with
regard to housing in Paris, based on an analysis of the results of the 1990 census.
Berger notes an outward residential spread of the metropolitan labour force and a
concomittant lowering of population density in Paris.

235 **Investment or family home? housing ownership in Paris at the turn**
of the twentieth century.
Marc H. Choko. *Journal of Urban History*, vol. 23 (July 1997),
p. 531-68. maps.
Choko uses statistical methods to support his hypothesis that between 1896 and 1901
homeowners in Paris were for the most part wealthy individuals who bought
apartment buildings as investments, not for living quarters.

236 **The state, housing policy and Afro-Caribbean migration to France.**
Stephanie A. Condon, Philip E. Ogden. *Ethnic and Racial Studies*,
vol. 16, no. 2 (April 1993), p. 236-97. bibliog.
A study of public housing policy in Paris and the Paris region in relation to
immigration from France's overseas departments. Using as their sources census data
and reports, as well as interviews with Afro-Caribbean women, the authors trace the
typical immigrant's Parisian housing odyssey from furnished accommodation to
public housing estate flats and, in some cases, to home ownership. Another recent
study of minorities and housing in Paris is 'The residential mobility of ethnic
minorities: a longitudinal analysis', by Catherine Bonvalet, Juliet Carpenter, Paul
White (*Urban Studies*, vol. 32 [Feb. 1995], p. 87-103).

237 **Women for hire; prostitution and sexuality in France after 1850.**
Alain Corbin, translated by Alan Sheridan.   Cambridge,
Massachusetts: Harvard University Press, 1990. 478p. bibliog.
A translation of *Filles de noce: misère sexuelle et prostitution aux 19e et 20e siècles*
(Paris: Aubier Montaigne, 1978). This insightful and influential book is often cited as
the best modern research on prostitution in France, in which Corbin separates truth
from folklore with regard to prostitution in Paris.

238 **From housing the poor to healing the sick: the changing institution
of Paris hospitals under the old regime and revolution.**
John Frangos.   Madison, New Jersey: Fairleigh Dickinson University
Press; London: Associated University Presses, 1997. 247p.
A history of institutional care in Paris during the 18th century.

239 **Bibliographie parisienne; tableaus de moeurs (1600-1880).**
Paul Lacombe, preface by Jules Cousin.   Paris: P. Rouquette, 1887.
249p.
A chronological list of 1,287 titles, indexed by author, on Parisian social life and
customs. This bibliography was compiled as part of a proposed 'Bibliographie
générale de Paris' (General bibliography of Paris), to be based on the collections of
the Bibliothèque Historique de la Ville de Paris.

240 **Money, morals, and manners: the culture of the French and
American upper-middle class.**
Michele Lamont.   Chicago: University of Chicago Press, 1992. 320p.
maps. (Morality and Society).
A cross-cultural study of the moral and ethical values of upper-middle-class white
males from Paris and Clermont-Ferrand compared with those of their American
counterparts in Indiana and New Jersey.

241 **Inner city poverty in Paris and London.**
Charles Madge, Peter Willmott.   London; Boston, Massachusetts:
Routledge & K. Paul, 1981. 133p. bibliog. (Reports of the Institute of
Community Studies).
A study of the social and economic conditions of disadvantaged Parisians, presented
in comparison with Londoners. Drawing on data gathered from North African manual
workers in the inner-city neighbourhood of Folie-Méricourt, the authors conclude that
housing inequality is more prevalent in Paris than in London. The study is interesting
in that its authors take into account more than income in their portrait of the poor in
the two cities.

242 **Housing the poor of Paris, 1850-1902.**
Ann-Louise Shapiro.   Madison, Wisconsin: University of Wisconsin
Press, 1985. 224p. bibliog.

A book based on the author's doctoral dissertation, 'Working class housing and public health in Paris, 1850-1902'. By the middle of the 19th century, both politicians and social reformers viewed unsanitary housing conditions in Paris as threatening to public health and the social order. The various plans advanced for solving the problems of housing the working class involved clashes between proponents of private enterprise and public housing.

Politics and
Administration

243 **Le régime administratif et financier de la ville de Paris et du
département de la Seine.** (The administrative and financial régime of
the City of Paris and the Department of the Seine.)
Paul Beaussier, François Debidour, Edgar Laparra.   Paris: La
Documentation Française, 1957-59. New ed. 4 vols. maps. (Le Monde
Contemporain).

The standard presentation of the administration of Paris. Earlier editions, entitled *Le
Régime Administratif et financier du Département de la Seine et de la ville de Paris*,
were prepared by Eugene Raiga and Maurice Felix (Paris: Rousseau & Cie., 1933; 2nd
ed. 1935-36).

244 **Paris lesbianism and the politics of reaction, 1900-1940.**
Shari Benstock.   In: *Hidden from history: reclaiming the gay and
lesbian past.*   Edited by Martin Bauml Duberman, Martha Vicinus,
George Chauncey, Jr.   New York: New American Library, 1989,
p. 332-46.

In this essay on the famous lesbian coteries of early 20th-century Paris, Benstock
examines the political commitments of Natalie Barney, Gertrude Stein, and Winifred
Bryher in the context of their sexual preferences. Benstock traces what she terms 'the
complex links among artistic practices, political ideologies, and sexual preferences'.
In particular, she finds that her study 'suggests that Natalie Barney's strong
identification with male power can be traced to both psychological and political roots
that contrast sharply with those of the wealthy, anti-Fascist Bryher'.

245   **Les finances de la ville de Paris de 1778 à 1900; suivies d'un essai de statistique comparative des dangers communales des principales villes françaises et étrangères de 1878 à 1898.** (The finances of the city of Paris from 1778 to 1900; followed by a comparative statistical essay on the communal dangers of the principal French and foreign towns between 1878 and 1898.)
Gason Cadoux.   Paris: Berger-Levrault, 1900. 821p. bibliog.
Washington, DC: Library of Congress, [n.d.]. 1 microfilm reel.
The standard history of public finance in Paris.

246   **The Paris ombudsman.**
Michel Junot.   In: *Human rights in urban areas*.   Paris: UNESCO, 1983, p. 127-31.
A paper presented at a UNESCO symposium in 1980 by Michel Junot, who held the office of Paris ombudsman at the time. Junot explains that the office of the ombudsman was established in 1970 in order to substitute a human being for a faceless bureaucratic administration. The majority of cases that the ombudsman deals with are in the area of human rights, and most often involve housing problems.

247   **The rise of the Paris red belt.**
Tyler Edward Stovall.   Berkeley, California: University of California Press, 1990. 249p. maps.
A case-study of the consolidation of Communist political culture in the 1920s and 1930s in the working-class suburb of Bobigny, northeast of Paris. Stovall first provides a general picture of the social history of metropolitan Paris, then concentrates on Bobigny where, according to Stovall, the Communist Party's deft handling of local issues was the key to its success in institutionalizing its political culture.

Economy

248 **The politics of women's work: the Paris garment trades, 1750-1915.**
Judith G. Coffin.   Princeton, New Jersey: Princeton University Press, 1996. 289p.

An economic history of the clothing trade and needlework industries in Paris which emphasizes the role played by women clothing workers.

249 **Paris-Ile de France in the 1990s: a European investment region.**
Thierry Cota, Veronique Dumont.   London: Economist Intelligence Unit, 1993. 100p. maps. bibliog. (Research Report no. M602).

A research report which forecasts economic conditions in the Paris region as an aid to investors.

250 **Dealers, critics, and collectors of modern painting: aspects of the Parisian art market between 1910 and 1930.**
Malcolm Gee.   New York: Garland Press, 1981. 300p. + 266p. bibliog. (Outstanding Dissertations in the Fine Arts).

A scholarly work on the Parisian market for paintings in the early 20th century, originally presented as the author's doctoral thesis at the University of London, 1977.

Transport

251 **Paris Metro: a century-long project.**
   Dave Clark. *Mass Transit*, vol. 21, no. 2 (March/April 1995),
   p. 20-22.
A brief history of the design and construction of the Paris underground railway
system.

252 **Preventing mass transit crime.**
   Edited by Ronald V. Clarke. Monsey, New York: Criminal Justice
   Press, 1996. 257p. maps. (Crime Prevention Studies, vol. 6).
This collection of essays includes a study by Nancy G. LaVigne, 'Designing for
security in Meteor: a projected new Metro line in Paris'.

253 **La Gare du Nord.**
   René Clozier. Paris: J.-B. Bailliere, 1940. 294p. maps.
Originally presented as the author's thesis at the University of Paris, Clozier's study,
in French, contains much useful information on Paris's northern railway terminus.

254 **Paris Métro handbook.**
   Brian Hardy. Harrow Weald, England: Capital Transport, 1988.
   104p. map.
The Paris underground railway was constructed by a group of civil engineers led by
Fulgence Bienvenue, who directed the project for forty years. Hardy's book is an
English-language guide to the system.

255 Paris underground.

Tamara Hovey.   New York: Orchard Books, 1991. 90p. bibliog.

This children's book on the Paris Metro traces the history of the system from 1900 to the present day. Hovey adds interest to her account with such topics as archaeological discoveries made during construction, underground disasters, and the use of the Metro during the Second World War. The book is illustrated with historical photographs.

256 Horse-drawn cabs and omnibuses in Paris: the idea of circulation and the business of public transit.

Nicholas Papayanis.   Baton Rouge, Louisiana: Louisiana State University Press, 1996. 217p.

A scholarly history of Parisian local transport, focusing on the development of the cab trade from 1855 to 1914.

Statistics

257 **Annuaire statistique de la Ville de Paris et des communes suburbaines de la Seine.** (Statistical annual of the city of Paris and the suburban communities of the Seine.)
Direction de Cabinet du Préfet. Préfecture de la Seine. Paris: Imprimerie National, 1881-1967. 88 vols.
From 1881 to 1967, this title was the official source for statistics on Paris: eighty-eight volumes were published, covering the years 1880 to 1967. After an interruption, this set was replaced by the yearly *Annuaire statistique*, 1982-91, published by the Direction des Finances de l'Etat et des Affaires Economiques; and then by the current annual statistical publication *Paris, chiffres* (Paris, figures) (Paris: Direction de l'urbanisme et des actions de l'Etat, Sous-Direction des affaires économiques, Bureau de l'action économique, 1992-).

258 **Recherches statistiques sur la ville de Paris et le Département de la Seine: recueil de tableaux dressés et réunis d'après les ordres de Monsieur le Comte de Chabrol, Conseiller d'Etat, Préfet du Département de la Seine.** (Statistical research on the city of Paris and the Department of the Seine: collection of tables drawn up and commissioned on the orders of Monsieur le Comte de Chabrol, State Advisor, Prefect of the Department of the Seine.)
Paris: Imprimerie Royale, 1821-60. 6 vols. maps; London: British Museum, 1970. 1 microfilm reel.
These volumes represent the first relatively complete gathering of statistical information on Paris. The first four volumes (vol 1: 1821; vol. 2: 1823; vol. 3: 1826; and vol. 4: 1829) were compiled under the direction of the Comte de Chabrol, prefect of Paris at the Restoration, and contain information going back to the 17th century. Later volumes were compiled under the direction of Comte de Rambuteau (vol. 5:

Statistics

1844) and Baron Haussmann (vol. 6: 1860). Statistics are provided on population, topography, police, administration, agriculture, consumption, industry, commerce, manufacture, and finance.

Education

259 **La Sorbonne: sa vie, son role, son oeuvre à travers les siècles.** (The Sorbonne: its life, its role, and its work through the centuries.)
Jean Bonnerot. Paris: Presses Universitaires de France, 1927. 232p.
A history of the University of Paris. This work is complemented by its author's later *L'université de Paris du moyen âge a nos jours* (The university of Paris from the Middle Ages to the present day) (Paris: Larousse, 1933. 222p.), a volume of illustrations depicting university life.

260 **Student life in the Quartier Latin, Paris.**
Clive Holland. *The Studio*, vol. 27, no. 115 (15 Oct. 1902), p. 33-40.
A fictionalized turn-of-the-century account of a typical art student ('Johnson [for so let us call him]') and how he spends his days as a *nouveau* in the Latin Quarter.

261 **What are condoms made of? a comparison between Clarkstown High School South in New York [state] and Lycée Jean de La Fontaine in Paris.**
Paul Klesnikov. *Forbes*, vol. 156 (11 Sept. 1995), p. 302-04.
An article that concludes that French secondary students outperform their American counterparts on reading and mathematics tests because teachers in Paris concentrate on the basic skills and uphold uncompromising standards.

262 **Paris and Oxford universities in the thirteenth and fourteenth centuries; an institutional and intellectual history.**
Gordon Leff. New York: Wiley, 1968. 331p. bibliog. (New Dimensions in History; Essays in Comparative History).
Focuses on the position occupied by the universities of Paris and Oxford in the intellectual life of Western Europe, and also on the the connection between the academic structure of each university and its intellectual activities. In the sections on

the Université de Paris, Leff provides interesting details regarding its faculties, curricula, regulations, teaching methods, etc., as well as information on such larger doctrinal and intellectual issues as Aristotelianism and Ockhamism.

263 **The Ecole Normale Supérieure and the Third Republic.**
Robert J. Smith. Albany, New York: State University of New York Press, 1982. 201p. bibliog.

Originally founded as a teacher-training college, the Ecole Normale Supérieure in Paris was destined to provide France with such leaders as Jaurés, Monod, Lavisse, and Herriot – men who dominated French politics during the Third Republic (1870-1940). In this scholarly study, Smith seeks the reasons for the emergence of the *normaliens* (students of the school) as a political and intellectual élite.

264 **Paula Li, Mohammed and their friends; immigrant schoolchildren in Paris.**
Ana Vasquez. *The UNESCO Courier*, vol. 44 (Oct. 91), p. 25-28.

This brief report on a multicultural class of Parisian schoolchildren emphasizes their success in crossing cultural boundaries and assimilating to French culture.

265 **The making of technological man: the social origins of French engineering education.**
John Hubbel Weiss. Cambridge, Massachusetts: MIT Press, 1982. 377p. bibliog.

A social and institutional history of the Parisian engineering school, the Ecole Centrale des Arts et Manufactures in Paris, from its founding in 1829 to 1848. Drawing on primary sources, Weiss provides information on such topics as the Ecole's pedagogical orientation and the social origins of its students.

Literature and Intellectual Life

General

266 **Americans in Paris, 1900-1930; a selected, annotated bibliography.**
William G. Bailey. Westport, Connecticut: Greenwood, 1989. 192p.
A bibliography of materials about the Americans who arrived in Paris during the early 20th century and about their expatriate experiences, both as bohemians and as serious artists.

267 **Women of the Left Bank, Paris, 1900-1940.**
Shari Benstock. Austin, Texas: University of Texas Press, 1986. 518p. bibliog.
Benstock has written a feminist critique of the work of literary women who took part in the Modernist movement in Paris during its heyday. Among the twenty-two women covered in the book are Natalie Barney, Djuna Barnes, Caresse Crosby, Sylvia Beach, H. D., Mina Loy, and Edith Wharton. Benstock emphasizes the lesbianism of many of her subjects.

268 **The atlas of literature.**
Edited by Malcolm Bradbury. London: De Agostini Editions, 1996. 352p. maps. bibliog.
A number of sections in this volume map the literary geography of Paris. They are: 'The Paris of the French Romantics', p. 70-03; 'The France of the Enlightenment', p. 38-41; 'Stendhal's, Balzac's and Sand's France', p. 92-95; 'Paris as Bohemia', p. 126-29; 'Paris in the Twenties', p. 174-77; and 'Existentialist Paris', p. 224-27.

269   **Exiled in Paris: Richard Wright, James Baldwin, Samuel Beckett and others on the Left Bank, 1946-60.**
James Campbell.   New York: Scribner, 1995. 271p. (Jamie Segall Collection in American Literature).

An examination of the expatriate Paris literary scene, post-Second World War to the early 1960s. This work is especially valuable for its presentation of the experiences of Afro-American writers who participated in the intellectual life of the *rive gauche*.

270   **La poésie de Paris dans la littérature française de Rousseau à Baudelaire.** (Parisian poetry in French literature from Rousseau to Baudelaire.)
Pierre Citron.   Paris: Editions de Minuit, 1961. 2 vols. bibliog.

A weighty analysis of the myth of Paris as it has persisted in French literature. Citron surveys the image of Paris in the entire range of French literature, but concentrates on the myth in the 18th and 19th centuries, particularly during the 1830-62 period. Citron concludes that two images of Paris were predominant during this era: Paris as a dynamic natural force; or Paris as a personification. An important feature of the volumes are separate chapters on Paris in the works of Balzac, Michelet, Hugo, Nerval, and Baudelaire.

271   **Les hauts lieux de la littérature à Paris.** (The high places of literature in Paris.)
Jean-Paul Clébert, photographs by Richard Lamoureux.   Paris: Bordas, 1992. 240p. maps. bibliog. (Collection Les Hauts Lieux. Littérature).

A richly detailed guide to the literary topography of Paris by a French expert. After an introductory chapter which provides a panoramic overview of Paris in relation to French literature, separate sections trace Parisian literature from Villon in the 15th century to the present day, identifying the places where French and a few European authors lived, wrote, worked, and wandered. Places linked to fictional events in literature are also noted.

272   **Nineteenth-century Paris: vision and nightmare.**
Peter Collier.   In: *Unreal city; urban experience in modern European literature and art.*   Edited by Edward Timms, David Kelley.   New York: St. Martin's Press, 1985, p. 25-44. bibliog.

An overview of 19th-century French artists and writers and the aesthetic approaches that they adopted to express the phenomenon of Paris. Collier discusses the work of such avant-garde artists and poets as Seurat, Manet, Toulouse-Lautrec, Alfred de Vigny, Baudelaire, Rimbaud, and Jules Laforgue.

273   **Paris on the eve, 1900-1914.**
Vincent Cronin.   New York: St. Martin's Press, 1991. 484p. bibliog.

The 'eve' is the eve of the First World War, and in this lively book for the general reader, Cronin's subject is the intellectual life of Paris 'from the turn of the nineteenth century until the beginning of the European War in 1914 [when] Paris was the scene of creative thinking and invention unusually rich in quantity and quality'. Cronin seeks to link and explain the creative achievements of the time and 'to present the period largely in terms of people'. To do so, he states that he has used recently published materials, especially with regard to André Gide, and also newspapers, periodicals, little magazines (journals produced outside the mainstream of publishing), and letters, as well as archival materials and interviews. Besides Gide, chapters are devoted to Paul Claudel, Marcel Proust, Pablo Picasso, Charles Péguy, and Claude Debussy. In his final chapter, Cronin brings the era to a close with 'Paris at War'.

274 **From Harlem to Paris: black American writers in France, 1840-1980.**
Michel Fabre.   Urbana, Illinois: University of Illinois Press, 1991. 358p. bibliog.

Fabre emphasizes biography in this well-documented presentation of the black American writers and intellectuals who responded to the stimulation of Parisian cultural life. Among his subjects are W. E. B. DuBois, Langston Hughes, Countee Cullen, Jessie Faust, Richard Wright, James Baldwin, Chester Himes and William Gardner Smith, as well as many lesser-known figures. Fabre is also the author of 'Richard Wright's Paris', in *The city in African-American literature*, edited by Yoshinobu Hakutani, Robert Butler (Madison, New Jersey: Fairleigh Dickinson University Press, 1995, p. 96-109).

275 **Paris as revolution; writing the nineteenth-century city.**
Priscilla Parkhurst Ferguson.   Berkeley, California: University of California Press, 1994. 261p.

Ferguson unites several disciplines in her stylish analysis of Paris as a cultural expression, an urban spatial narrative. She centres her discussion around the idea of Revolution – 'a virtuoso metaphor' – as played out imaginatively in the literature of the 19th century and dramatized in actuality in the 19th-century reconstruction of the city. Drawing on material selected from contemporary journalism, essays, guidebooks ('proto-novels'), as well as the depiction of Parisian life in such novels as *L'éducation sentimentale* (Flaubert); *Paris, La Curée,* and *La Débâcle* (Zola); *Quatrevingt-treize* (Hugo); and *L'Insurgé* (Vallès), Ferguson demonstrates how 19th-century literature charted the course of France's defining political event, the Revolution, and in so doing, redefined the Parisian representational 'landscape'.

276 **Sylvia Beach and the Lost Generation: a history of literary Paris in the Twenties and Thirties.**
Noel Riley Fitch.   New York: Norton, 1983; London: Souvenir Press, 1984. 447p.

A biography of Sylvia Beach, proprietor of the Paris bookshop Shakespeare and Company, who was a key figure in literary Paris in the *entre-deux-guerres* period, and is perhaps best known as the publisher of James Joyce's *Ulysses* in 1922. Besides drawing upon Beach's own memoirs, *Shakespeare and Company* (London: Faber & Faber, 1959. 232p.), Fitch had access to the Beach family papers in preparing this work, which centres on the bookshop and Joyce.

277 **Imagining Paris; exile, writing, and American identity.**
J. Gerald Kennedy. New Haven, Connecticut: Yale University Press, 1993. 269p. map.

Kennedy explores the Parisian lives of five American writers – Gertrude Stein, Ernest Hemingway, Henry Miller, Scott Fitzgerald, and Djuna Barnes – highlighting their psychological struggles to accommodate contradictory expatriate and American identities, the experience that Kennedy identifies as central to their literary work.

278 **Thresholds of a new world; intellectuals and the exile experience in Paris, 1830-1848.**
Lloyd S. Kramer. Ithaca, New York: Cornell University Press, 1988. 297p. bibliog.

This is a study in intellectual history, an analysis, as the author states in his introduction, 'of the social and intellectual reality of exile in nineteenth-century France'. Kramer examines the experience of exile in July Monarchy Paris (1830-48) in connection with the ideas of three Europeans who left their own countries for Paris: the German Heinrich Heine, who lived in Paris from 19 May 1831, until his death in 1856; the German Karl Marx, who resided in Paris from October 1843, until expelled by the French government in February 1845; and the Pole Adam Mickiewicz, who arrived in Paris in August 1832 and lived there the rest of his life. Kramer's analysis of these men in the Parisian milieu nicely captures the ferment of ideas in Paris and its influence on these three Europeans.

279 **We all went to Paris; Americans in the City of Light, 1776-1971.**
Stephen Longstreet. New York: Macmillan, 1972. 448p.

In his 'Introduction', Longstreet states that he intends his book to be 'a story for the intelligent reader', about 'a representative assortment of [American] men and women' and their life in Paris. Longstreet presents some unusual but undocumented information, emphasizing the love affairs and sexual adventures of his subjects. The reader will be entertained by anecdotes about Benjamin Franklin, Robert Fulton, George Catlin, James Whistler, Anna Gould, Henry James, Mary Cassatt, Edith Wharton, John Singer Sargent, Gertrude Stein, and Isadora Duncan, to name only a few of the many Americans included in the book. An index would have added to the book's usefulness.

280 **Three literary visions of seventeenth-century Paris.**
Louis A. MacKenzie, Jr. In: *Literary generations; a festschrift in honor of Edward D. Sullivan by his friends, colleagues, and former students.* Edited by Alain Toumayan. Lexington, Kentucky: French Forum, 1992, p. 98-109.

MacKenzie compares the treatment of Paris in the poetry of Saint-Amant with the literary visions of the city imparted in Boileau's *Satires* and La Bruyere's *Les caractères*.

281 **The Paris of the novelists.**
Arthur Bartlett Maurice. New York: Doubleday, Page & Co., 1919.
299p. Reprinted, Port Washington, New York: Kennikat Press, 1973.
The Paris of the novelists that Maurice treats in this book is both the Paris in which
they lived and the Paris of which they wrote. The first part of this book devotes
separate chapters to Paris in the lives and in the fictional works of Victor Hugo,
William Thackeray and Charles Dickens, Alexandre Dumas, Honoré de Balzac,
Alphonse Daudet, Emile Zola, and Guy de Maupassant. Mention is also made of Paris
in the works of, among others, Eugene Sue, Emile Gaboriau, George Du Maurier, and
a number of British and American novelists.

282 **Paris in American literature.**
Jean Meral, translated from the French by Laurette Long. Chapel
Hill, North Carolina: University of North Carolina Press, 1989. 284p.
bibliog.
A shortened version of Meral's *Paris dans la littérature américaine* (Paris: CNRS,
1983). Writing for the general reader, Meral focuses on two major themes that he
identifies as having obsessed Americans writing about Paris from Edgar Allan Poe to
James Baldwin: exoticism and the expatriate experience.

283 **American expatriate writing and the Paris moment: modernism
and place.**
Donald Pizer. Baton Rouge, Louisiana: Louisiana State University,
1996. 149p. bibliog. (Modernist Studies).
The author describes his book as a study of the 'mythic Paris' of French modernism.
He focuses on the influence this concept exerted on the literature of American self-
exile in Paris during the 1920s and 1930s. The authors covered are Ernest
Hemingway, Gertrude Stein, Anais Nin, John Dos Passos, Henry Miller, and Scott
Fitzgerald.

284 **Paris in the nineteenth century.**
Christopher Prendergast. Oxford; Cambridge, Massachusetts:
Blackwell, 1992. 283p.
A study of the representational life of Paris; that is, how the cityscape was 'written' in
the literature of 19th-century France. Prendergast examines how the man-made
environment was appropriated, depicted, and transfigured in Lautreamont's *Les chants
de Maldoror*, Zola's *La Curée*, Flaubert's *L'éducation sentimentale*, and Hugo's *Les
Misérables*, as well as in the paintings of Manet and Van Gogh. Readers will find this
a demanding but rewarding book.

285 **Les salons littéraires parisiens du Second Empire à nos jours.**
(Parisian literary salons from the Second Empire to the present day.)
Laure Riese. Toulouse, France: Privat, 1962. 271p.
A presentation of more than 100 literary salons that contributed to the intellectual life
of Paris.

286   **The continual pilgrimage; American writers in Paris, 1944-1960.**
Christopher Sawyer-Laucanno.   New York: Grove Press, 1992. 345p.

A literary history of the post-Second World War wave of American writers drawn to Paris as a mecca of art and culture. Among those profiled in the book are Richard Wright, James Baldwin, William Styron, James Jones, Chester Himes, George Plimpton, John Ashbery, Harry Mathews, Allen Ginsberg, Lawrence Ferlinghetti, Alexander Trocchi, and William Burroughs.

287   **Paris noir: African Americans in the City of Light.**
Tyler Stovall.   Boston, Massachusetts: Houghton Mifflin, 1996. 366p.

A chronicle of the black American expatriates who joined their white American counterparts in Paris from the 1920s to the post-Second World War era. These include not only writers, such as Richard Wright, James Baldwin, and Claude McKay, but also jazz musicians, dancers, painters, and artists. Stovall examines both the influence of Paris on African-American creativity and also the contributions black Americans made to the French capital.

288   **Colour studies in Paris.**
Arthur Symons.   London: Chapman & Hall; New York: E. P. Duttton, 1918. 223p.

Symons's essays on late 19th-century Paris cover such topics as Montmartre and the Latin Quarter, Comte Robert de Montesquiou, Yvette Guilbert, the Moulin Rouge, Victor Hugo, Petrus Borel, Paul Verlaine, and Odilon Redon. The volume is illustrated with portraits and cartoons.

Individuals

Apollinaire

289   **Defeat and rebirth: the city poetry of Apollinaire.**
David Kelley.   In: *Unreal city; urban experience in modern European literature and art.*   Edited by Edward Timms, David Kelley.   New York: St. Martin's Press, 1985, p. 80-96.

Kelley illustrates the importance of Paris in Apollinaire's work and 'the complex ambivalence of his attitude towards [the city]' by explicating two poems by the poet, 'Zone' and 'Vendemiaire', poems that open and close *Alcools* (1913), the first major collection of Apollinaire's poetry. Kelley also points out some interesting parallels between Apollinaire's poetry and the paintings of Pablo Picasso.

Louis Aragon

290   **The Surrealist map of love.**
       Michel Beaujour. *Yale French Studies*, vol. 32 (1964), p. 124-32.
Beaujour writes that 'what the young Surrealists termed their "modernity" is a peculiar way of manifesting their Parisian essence . . . Paris is [for the Surrealists] the hub of the universe'. Beaujour proceeds to analyse the place of Paris in Aragon's *Le Paysan de Paris* (The peasant of Paris) and in the work of other members of the Surrealist group, particularly with regard to the central Surrealist myth of erotic Paris: in the Surrealists' texts, Paris 'is a zone . . . where love, in its multiple forms, beckons, hypnotizes and transforms the life of the seeker'.

291   **Surrealist city narrative: Breton and Aragon.**
       Peter Collier. In: *Unreal city; urban experience in modern European literature and art.* Edited by Edward Timms, David Kelley. New York: St. Martin's Press, 1985, p. 214-29.
Collier compares and contrasts Louis Aragon's *Paysan de Paris* (The peasant of Paris) (1926) and André Breton's *Nadja* (1928) as examples of the Surrealistic depiction of Paris. He analyses how Aragon and Breton both construct prose structures that map their narrators' fantasies and desires onto a Paris that ultimately eludes them.

Paris and the Surrealists.
See item no. 300.

Honoré de Balzac

292   **Balzac, 'archéologue' de Paris.** (Balzac, 'archaeologist' of Paris.)
       Jeannine Guichardet.   Paris: Sedes, 1986. 497p. maps. bibliog.
In this work, originally presented as a doctoral thesis at the Sorbonne in 1982, Guichardet explores the connections between Balzac's Parisian home and haunts and the Parisian background against which the 'Comédie humaine' unfolds: her book is both criticism and a guide to Balzacian landmarks. Two other books in French that deal with Balzac's treatment of Paris in his cycle of novels are *Le Paris de 'la Comédie Humaine'; Balzac et ses fournisseurs* (The Paris of 'la Comédie Humaine'; Balzac and his suppliers) by Henri Clouzot and R.-H. Valensi (Paris: Le Goupy, 1926. 192p.) and *Paris dans la Comédie humaine de Balzac* (Paris in the Comédie humaine by Balzac) by Norah W. Stevenson (Paris: G. Courville, 1938. 238p.).

293   **Balzac's heaven and hell.**
       Michel Philip. *Yale French Studies*, no. 32 (1964), p. 77-81.
Noting that Balzac lived in Paris and found in the city the characters and setting for his fiction, Philip points out that Balzac worked with the reality of Paris to give it meaning in his novels: everything in Balzac's fictional capital appears as necessary; nothing is merely anecdotal.

294 **Framing the city: two Parisian windows.**
Christopher Prendergast. In: *City images: perspectives from
literature, philosophy, and film.* Edited by Mary-Ann Caws. New
York: Gordon & Breach, 1991, p. 179-95.

Compares Balzac's treatment of Paris in his novels with the Paris depicted in
Baudelaire's poetry.

295 **Guide to Balzac's Paris; an analytical subject index.**
George B. Raser. Choisy-le-Roi, France: Imprimerie de France,
1964. 185p. map. bibliog.

A selective subject index to Balzac's references to Paris in his *Comédie humaine.* In
his 'Introduction', Raser characterizes his book as a 'methodical index or *"table
raisonee"* '. Raser first lists references to Paris in general, then, references to the
specific quarters, streets, houses, portions of public buildings, etc., mentioned in
Balzac's series of novels. The material is presented in fourteen major categories: outer
Left-Bank faubourgs; outer Right-Bank faubourgs; Left-Bank districts of poverty and
indigence; the small tradespeople; 'le XIIIe arrondissement'; Latin Quarter; the
average bourgeoisie or annuitants; the richer bourgeoisie; the financial quarter; the
Faubourg Saint-Germain; La Cité; the Boulevards; the theatres; and the Palais-Royal.

296 **The heart of Balzac's Paris.**
George B. Raser. Choisy-le-Roi, France: Imprimerie de France,
1970. 103p.

In three sections entitled 'The Boulevards', 'The Theaters', and 'The Palais-Royal',
Raser examines each of these milieux to determine Balzac's use of the Parisian
environment to realistically depict and artfully suggest the characters of his novelistic
personae.

Guide de Paris mystérieux. (Guide to secret Paris.)
See item no. 34.

The atlas of literature.
See item no. 268.

Charles Baudelaire

297 **Baudelaire: city images and the dream of stone.**
Victor Brombert. *Yale French Studies*, no. 32 (1964), p. 99-105.

Brombert describes Baudelaire as Paris's 'ironic *flâneur*, the ubiquitous observer, the
explorer of a mystery ... the haunted traveler in a world of phantoms, an ailing
prophet roaming through the cosmopolis-inferno'. Brombert points out the dominant
images of Paris in Baudelaire's poetry: images of rain, fog, and spectres. Baudelaire's
city is a nocturnal Paris 'of crime and hospital anguish', but above all, a city of stone,
symbolizing Baudelaire's hatred of nature.

Framing the city: two Parisian windows.
See item no. 294.

Manet and the Paris of Haussmann and Baudelaire.
See item no. 328.

Walter Benjamin

298 **Profane illumination; Walter Benjamin and the Paris of the Surrealist Revolution.**
Margaret Cohen.   Berkeley, California: University of California Press, 1993. 271p. bibliog. (Weimar and Now, no. 5).

A scholarly critique of Benjamin's Marxist philosophy that emphasizes the important position that Surrealist texts, in particular the Parisian panorama displayed in André Beton's *Nadja*, occupied in Benjamin's thought.

299 **Facades; Walter Benjamin's Paris.**
Anne Higonnet, Margaret Higonnet, Patrice Higonnet.   *Critical Inquiry*, vol. 10, no. 3 (March 1984), p. 391-419.

A scholarly critique of Walter Benjamin's 'Paris, capital of the nineteenth century' written in 1935 in *Reflections; essays, aphorisms, autobiographical writings*, translated from the German by Edmund Jephcott, edited and with an introduction by Peter Demetz (New York: Harcourt, Brace, Jovanovich, 1978, p. 146-62). Benjamin's essay is characterized by the authors of this article as 'our most prestigious study of the culture of nineteenth-century Europe ... an elliptical expose of Benjamin's projected book *Arcades (Passagen)*, the magnum opus left incomplete in his briefcase at his tragic suicide on the Spanish border in 1940'. According to the authors of this study, Benjamin saw Paris as 'the locus classicus of bourgeois culture, which finds its most conspicuous expresssion in the arcade', and the leitmotif of the facade is central to Benjamin's analysis of 19th-century Paris.

André Breton

300 **Paris and the Surrealists.**
George Melly, photography by Michael Woods.   New York: Thames & Hudson, 1991. 159p.

An introduction both to the creators and practitioners of Surrealism – in particular André Breton and Louis Aragon – and to the Paris background which was central to the literary movement. Melly's text interprets the Surrealists' ambiguous city which is strikingly presented in more than 100 photographs.

Surrealist city narrative: Breton and Aragon.
See item no. 291.

Profane illumination; Walter Benjamin and the Paris of the Surrealist Revolution.
See item no. 298.

Julien Green

301 **Paris.**
Julien Green, with an English translation by J. A. Underwood, photographs by Julien Green.   New York; London: Boyars, 1991. bilingual ed. 160p.

These nineteen literary essays written by Green about his favourite places in Paris can be read as elegiac prose poems or as a guidebook to Julien Green's Paris. The essays are presented with French texts and English translations on facing pages. Green's own photographs intensify his evocative descriptions of the city.

Heinrich Heine

302 **The poet dying: Heinrich Heine's last years in Paris.**
Ernst Pawel.   New York: Farrar, Straus & Giroux, 1995. 277p.

A biographical study of the German poet, whose last years were spent in exile in Paris. Although Heine was bed-ridden from 1848 and partially blind, the poetic meditations he composed at the end of his life are considered his finest work. Pawel describes the various apartments which Heine occupied in Paris and his daily routine, detailing Heine's everyday life against a background of the political situation in France and Germany.

Thresholds of a new world; intellectuals and the exile experience in Paris, 1830-1848.
See item no. 278.

Ernest Hemingway

303 **Hemingway's Paris.**
Compiled by Robert E. Gajdusek.   New York: Scribner, 1978. 182p. bibliog.

In this book, Gajdusek brings together pictures of Ernest Hemingway's Parisian milieu with quotations by and about the American expatriate. Hemingway *aficionados* will find that this book serves as a visual index to connections between the writer's work and Parisian scenes.

304   **Less than a treason: Hemingway in Paris.**
      Peter Griffen.   New York: Oxford University Press, 1990. 197p.
This book follows *Along with youth* (New York: Oxford University Press, 1985.
258p.), and is the second volume of Griffen's biography of Ernest Hemingway.
Griffen details the writer's early Parisian years, at the time when Hemingway had
written *The sun also rises* and was a member of the group of American expatriates that
included Gertrude Stein, Ezra Pound, and Scott Fitzgerald. Another book dealing with
this period is Michael Reynolds's *Hemingway: the Paris years* (Oxford; Cambridge,
Massachusetts: Blackwell, 1989. 356p.).

Walks in Hemingway's Paris: a guide to Paris for the literary traveler.
See item no. 44.

A moveable feast.
See item no. 214.

Victor Hugo

305   **Paris dans *Les misérables*.**
      Claudette Combes.   Nantes, France: CID Editions, 1981. 338p. maps.
      bibliog.
A detailed study and meticulous reconstruction of the Paris of *Les Misérables*, a city
imaginatively elaborated by Hugo. Interested general readers as well as specialists will
find this study extremely useful. Maps and photographs clarify Combes's text.

306   **The mysteries of Paris and London.**
      Richard Maxwell.   Charlottesville, Virginia: University Press of
      Virginia, 1992. 415p. bibliog. (Victorian Literature and Culture
      Series).
A scholarly inquiry into a literary genre that the author of this book describes as 'the
novel of urban mysteries'. The focus of Maxwell's critique is on London as depicted
in the novels of Charles Dickens, but two of Victor Hugo's novels are also examined
as examples of the genre. Maxwell devotes two chapters to Hugo and Paris: 'The
Labyrinths of Notre-Dame', and 'Mystery and revelation in *Les misérables*'.

307   **Capitale de la violence: Le Paris de Victor Hugo.** (Capital of
      violence: the Paris of Victor Hugo.)
      Jacques Seebacher.   *Cahiers de l'Association International des
      Etudes Françaises*, vol. 42 (May 1990), p. 31-46.
A study of Hugo's use of politics and revolution in his Paris fiction.

Guide de Paris mystérieux. (Guide to secret Paris.)
See item no. 34.

Thomas Jefferson

308 **Thomas Jefferson's Paris.**
Howard C. Rice, Jr.   Princeton, New Jersey: Princeton University
Press, 1976. 156p. maps.

An outstanding volume and a model of creative scholarship. Rice's objective is to
recreate 'in words and pictures the city of Paris as Jefferson knew it under the reign of
Louis XVI'. Jefferson was a representative of the American government in France
from 1784 to 1789, first serving as a commissioner and then, in March 1785,
succeeding Benjamin Franklin as a minister. During this time, he grew to know Paris
and the Parisians well. 'Perlustration' was Jefferson's word for exploration. In this
book, Rice and his readers 'perlustrate' 18th-century Paris in Jefferson's footsteps.
Taking his 'clues from Jefferson's letters, travel memoranda, and account books',
Rice reconstructs Jefferson's sojourn in the city, bringing together in this book 180
illustrations of Parisian sights as Jefferson saw them (and, in some cases, as they look
today). Besides showing the scenes that caught Jefferson's eye, Rice provides a
scholarly text that traces the events of Jefferson's life in Paris and identifies the people
with whom he came into contact.

James Joyce

309 **Joyce the Parisian.**
Jean-Michel Rebate.   In: *Cambridge companion to James Joyce.*
Edited by Derek Attridge.   New York: Cambridge University Press,
1990, p. 83-102.

Paris played a special role in the life of the self-exiled Irish writer James Joyce, both
as a powerful myth and as the place where he lived and worked for two decades
during the *entre-deux-guerres* period. Rebate's article explores both these aspects of
Joyce's relation to the city. On p. 88 the reader will find a list of Joyce's Parisian
addresses, 1920-39.

Henry Miller

310 **Henry Miller: the Paris years.**
Brassai, translated from the French by Timothy Bent, with photographs
by the author.   Berkeley, California: Arcade Pub, 1995. 224p. map.

The autobiographical basis of Henry Miller's novels is well-known. In this book, the
Hungarian-born photographer Robert Brassai, who met Miller in the early 1930s,
offers his version of events that occurred in Paris and which were later transferred by
Miller to his fiction. Brassai's reminiscences of his friendship with Miller are
enhanced by the inclusion of sixteen of Brassai's photographs of Paris. This book was
first published in Paris in 1975 as *Henry Miller, grandeur nature* (Paris: Gallimard,
1975).

Marcel Proust

311 **Proust's beloved enemy.**
Jack Murray. *Yale French Studies*, vol. 32 (1964), p. 112-17.
Murrary points out that in *A la recherche du temps perdu*, 'Paris is [for Proust's protagonist Marcel] . . . the scene of continual disenchantment, disgust, or despair as Marcel explores [his] dream-worlds in their concrete and actual form'. At the same time, in Proust's own life, 'Paris was the scene of a titanic struggle . . . a struggle in which Proust was not only victorious but also infinitely enhanced by the impressive stature of [Paris] his beloved enemy'.

Rainer Maria Rilke

312 **Le Paris de Rainer Maria Rilke.** (The Paris of Rainer Maria Rilke.)
Jacques Dugast. *Europe; Revue Littéraire Mensuelle*, vol. 67, no. 719 (March 1989), p. 75-87.
Dugast discusses both Rilke's imaginative and biographical relationship to Paris.

313 **Paris/childhood: the fragmented body in Rilke's** *Notebooks of Malte Laurids Brigge*.
Andreas Huyssen. In: *Modernity and the text; revisions of German modernism*. Edited by Andreas Huyssen, David Bathrick. New York: Columbia University Press, 1989, p. 131-41.
Explores the treatment of Paris in Rilke's novel.

314 **Rilke's Paris – 'cité pleine de rêves'.**
Naomi Segal. In: *Unreal city; urban experience in modern European literature and art*. Edited by Edward Timms, David Kelley. New York: St. Martin's Press, 1985, p. 97-110.
The author of this article argues that when 'Rilke arrived in Paris in August 1902 . . . he was not only alone but also suddenly and violently confronted by an overwhelming material environment'. The powerful impression of Paris that Rilke received at this time was recreated in his work, most successfully in an aesthetic sense in his *Aufzeichnungen des Malte Laurids Brigge* (The notebooks of Malte Laurids Brigge) in which his anxiety, hallucinations, and fears found expression in a depiction of Paris that is, in Segal's words, 'childhood corrupted into adult nightmare'.

The flâneur.
See item no. 7.

Jean-Paul Sartre

315 **Sartre's ambiguous friend.**
     Annie Cecchi. *Yale French Studies*, no. 32 (1964), p. 133-37.

According to Cecchi, Sartre's Paris is 'a presence, not a myth'. In his novels, Sartre offers his readers a familiar and domestic city, an everyday Paris, neither exalted nor mysterious. In this article, Cecchi analyses Sartre's feelings about the city where he spent much of his life, and shows how his experience of Paris is expressed in his novels.

Stendhal

316 **Paris au temps de Stendhal: [exposition], Mairie de Paris.** (Paris
     during Stendhal's time: [exhibition], Paris Town Hall.)
     Edited by the Association des Amis de Stendhal. Paris: Association
     des Amis de Stendhal, 1983. 62p.

The catalogue of an exhibition held at the Mairie de Paris. Stendhal arrived in Paris on 10 November 1799 (19 Brumaire) and spent seventeen years of his life there, dying in Paris on 21 March 1842. The materials assembled for this exhibition ably link Stendhal with his two Parises, the autobiographical and the imagined. Besides the main text, 'Paris au temps de Stendhal', the volume contains a detailed chronology of Stendhal's life and a chronology of events in Paris, from 1800 to 1842.

The atlas of literature.
See item no. 268.

Emile Zola

317 **Zola's city.**
     Kenneth Cornell. *Yale French Studies*, vol. 32 (1964), p. 106-11.

According to the author of this essay, Zola early 'conceived the idea of making Paris a kind of character in a novel, giving the city a role analogous to the Greek chorus of tragedy'. In this article, Cornell points out how Zola incorporated Paris into his novels through such methods as panoramic descriptions, aerial vantage points, and personification of the city. Cornell concludes, 'In the final analysis, Paris the monster is his constant image'.

318 **Paris dans les romans d'Emile Zola.** (Paris in the novels of Emile
     Zola.)
     Nathan Kranowski. Paris: Presses Universitaires de France, 1968.
     159p. bibliog.

Originally submitted as the author's thesis at Columbia University in 1966 under the title *Paris in the works of Emile Zola; a study of urban poetry and mores in his novels*, this scholarly work is largely an analysis of Zola's use of Paris in *Les Rougon-*

Macquart. Kranowski identifies Zola's principal image of Paris as a romantic personification of the city: portraying Paris as a gigantic human being allows Zola to dramatize the city itself.

The Arts

Visual arts

319   **The Academy and French painting in the nineteenth century.**
Albert Boime.   London: Phaidon; New York: Praeger, 1971. 330p.
bibliog.

A ground-breaking volume that reoriented the study of 19th-century French painting.
In this book, Boime re-examines the role played by the Académie des Beaux-Arts in
Paris in regard to the painting of the 1830-80 era, and demonstrates that the academic
training that artists of the time received in the Ecole des Beaux-Arts contributed to,
rather than stultified, their painting. Chapters cover the 19th-century idea of 'official
art' and the instruction imparted to art students in Paris, both in private ateliers and in
the studios of the Ecole des Beaux-Arts.

320   **Art and the French Commune; imagining Paris after war and
revolution.**
Albert Boime.   Princeton, New Jersey: Princeton University Press,
1995. 234p. maps. (The Princeton Series in Nineteenth-Century Art,
Culture, and Society).

In this erudite and absorbing monograph, Boime argues that the art of Impressionism
had political roots in the need for the Parisian bourgeoisie to erase the memory of
working-class socialism and the violence of the Paris Commune and 'retake' Paris
symbolically. In support of his hypothesis, Boime closely examines the visual images
of the time, from Impressionist paintings to periodical illustrations.

321   **Van Gogh à Paris; Musée d'Orsay, 2 février-15 mai 1988.** (Van
      Gogh in Paris; Musée d'Orsay, 2 February-15 May 1988.)
      Françoise Cachin, Bogmila Welsh-Ovcharov, with contributions by
      Monique Nonne [et al.].   Paris: Ministère de la culture et de la
      communication/Editions de la Réunion des Musées Nationaux, 1988.
      403p. bibliog.

Vincent van Gogh produced some of his best known paintings during the two years –
from March 1886 to February 1888 – that he lived in Paris. This volume is a catalogue
of those paintings, accompanied by essays about his work. A chapter entitled 'Amis et
Contemporains de Van Gogh' (Friends and contemporaries of Van Gogh) explores
Van Gogh's connection with the Paris art world of such painters as Sisley, Pissarro,
and Renoir, along with reproductions of the paintings of these and other artists of the
time.

322   **The painting of modern life, Paris in the art of Manet and his
      followers.**
      T. J. Clark.   New York: Knopf, 1985. 338p. bibliog.

A seminal work in the study of the Impressionist art movement. Clark centres his
study on the painting of Edouard Manet (1832-83) and those he influenced, and
interprets their artistic depiction of Paris in the light of the social structures, values,
and attitudes which were characteristic of Paris in the latter half of the 19th century.

323   **Olympia: Paris in the age of Manet.**
      Otto Friedrich.   New York: Harper Collins, 1992. 329p.

Friedrich places painter Edouard Manet and his controversial art at the centre of this
cultural history of Paris in the 19th century. Among those discussed in the book are
Manet's fellow artists (Degas, Monet, Morisot), his friends and defenders (Baudelaire,
Zola), his models, and such political figures as Napoleon III and the Empress Eugénie.

324   **Léger and purist Paris.**
      Edited by John Golding, Christopher Green.   London: Tate Gallery,
      1971. 108p. bibliog.

This catalogue of an exhibition held at the Tate Gallery, London, 18 November
1970-24 January 1971, contains reproductions of the paintings of Fernand Léger
(1881-1955) that capture the Parisian cityscape in the clear, flat colours of the Purist
movement.

325   **Impressionism: art, leisure, and Parisian society.**
      Robert L. Herbert.   New Haven, Connecticut: Yale University Press,
      1988. 324p. maps. bibliog.

A scholarly study of the social context in which the Parisian art movement known as
Impressionism took shape and flourished from the 1860s to the mid-1880s. Organized
topically, the book illuminates Impressionist paintings with the aid of social history,
the 311 illustrations in the volume serving as an index to the Impressionists'
brilliantly-depicted Paris. In his annotated bibliography, Herbert comments on books
dealing with the Impressionist decades.

326 **Kiki's Paris: artists and lovers, 1900-1930.**
Billy Kluver, Julie Martin. New York: Abrams, 1989. 263p. bibliog.
Reprinted, 1994.
A lavishly illustrated biography of the artists' model Kiki (1901-53) and the artists
and intellectuals – among them Man Ray, Léger, Miro, Modigliani, Brancusi, Calder,
and Cocteau – who shared her Montparnasse world.

327 **Paris without end; on French art since World War I.**
Jed Perl. San Francisco: North Point, 1988. 146p.
Perl provides separate essays on the artists of the School of Paris – Matisse, Derain,
Dufy, Léger, Picasso, Braque, Giacometti, Helion, and Balthus – who worked in
France from the 1920s to the 1970s. He traces their development and re-evaluates
their work. The book is illustrated with fifty black-and-white reproductions.

328 **Manet and the Paris of Haussmann and Baudelaire.**
Theodore Reff. In: *Visions of the modern city; essays in history, art,
and literature.* Edited by William Sharpe, Leonard Wallock. New
York: Columbia University, 1983, p. 131-63.
Edouard Manet, a painter and also a Parisian born and bred, was sensitive to the visual
effects of Haussmann's drastic transformation of his city. In this article Reff records
Manet's aesthetic response to the 'Haussmannization' of 19th-century Paris.

329 **The murals of Eugène Delacroix at Saint-Sulpice.**
Jack J. Spector. New York: College Art Association of America,
1967. 171p. (Monographs on Archaeology and Fine Arts, no. 16).
Between 1849 and 1861, Eugène Delacroix (1798-1863) painted three murals on the
walls of Saint-Sulpice in Paris: *Heliodorus Driven from the Temple, Jacob Wrestling
with the Angel*, and *St. Michael Vanquishing Lucifer*. In this scholarly monograph,
Spector discusses these murals in detail, analysing Delacroix's compositions to
determine how the painter achieved his effects.

330 **The lure of Paris; nineteenth-century American painters and their
French teachers.**
H. Barbara Weinberg. New York: Abbeville Press, 1991. 295p.
bibliog.
A splendid book with full-page and double-page illustrations that combines an
attractive large format with exceptional scholarship. After the American Civil War,
American art students flocked to Paris: Weinberg explores this migration and the
impact of French art training on late 19th-century American painting. After first
presenting a general survey of her subject, she discusses such topics as the Ecole des
Beaux-Arts, the Salons, and art instruction at the atelier of Parisian painter Jean-Leon
Gêrome. The volume is thoroughly documented from archival materials, books,
catalogues, dissertations, journal articles, pamphlets, and unpublished papers.

331 **The city in painting.**
Frank Whitford. In: *Unreal city; urban experience in modern European literature and art.* Edited by Edward Timms, David Kelley. New York: St. Martin's Press, 1985, p. 45-64.
Whitford discusses the painting of Parisian street scenes by such artists as Monet, Cézanne, and Robert Delaunay, comparing and contrasting these French artists' visions of Paris with the expression of city life in the work of Italian and German painters.

Decorative arts

332 **Paris interiors; interieurs parisiens.**
Lisa Lovatt-Smith, edited by Angelika Muthesius. Koln, Germany: Taschen, 1994. 339p.
More than 400 colour illustrations, accompanied by a trilingual text (English, French, and German), display the multitude of decorative styles chosen by Parisians for their private homes and apartments.

333 **Tout Paris: the source guide to the art of French decoration.**
Patricia Twohill Lown, David Lown, illustrated by Françoise McAree. St. Helier, Jersey: Palancar Co., 1994. 410p.
This classified directory to the decorative arts and artisans in Paris comprises more than 2,000 entries, each consisting of address, telephone and fax numbers, and a brief commentary.

334 **The rococo interior: decoration and social space in early eighteenth-century Paris.**
Katie Scott. New Haven, Connecticut: Yale University Press, 1995. 342p.
A visually delightful book as well as an interdisciplinary scholarly study that will be required reading for all students of 18th-century Paris. While Scott has written an art history of rococo decoration in *ancien régime* Paris, she has also established a broad explanatory framework linking the rococo with political, social, and economic aspects of the 18th century, making her book of interest to scholars in many fields.

The birth of intimacy: privacy and domestic life in early modern Paris.
See item no. 99.

Photography

335 **Paris: the city and its photographers.**
Patrick Deedes-Vincke. Boston, Massachusetts: Little, Brown, 1992.
144p. (A Bullfinch Press Book).
Deedes-Vincke covers the entire history of photography in Paris from its beginnings
in 1839 to 1968, making connections between the art form and the city. He begins
with the experimentation of Daguerre, then covers the artistic photography of Atget,
Kertesz, and Cartier-Bresson, the photojournalism of Capa, and, finally, the
commercialism of contemporary Parisian photographers. The book is well-illustrated,
providing a tour of Paris as well as narrating the history of Parisian photography.

336 **Industrial madness: commercial photography in Paris, 1848-1871.**
Elizabeth Anne McCauley. New Haven, Connecticut: Yale
University Press, 1994. 448p. bibliog. (Yale Publications in the History
of Art).
McCauley begins with a general overview of Paris's 19th-century photography
industry and the social world in which the city's commercial photographers practised
their trade. She then furnishes case-studies of the Paris studios of photographers
Nadar, Braquehais, Collard, and Aubry. McCauley has gathered together much
fascinating information for her book, covering such aspects of the photography
industry as pornography and art reproductions for the masses.

337 **Souvenirs.**
Shelley Rice. *Art in America*, vol. 76, no. 9 (Sept. 1988), p. 156-71.
A scholarly, heavily-documented article on the photographs taken by Felix Nadar
(1820-1910) during the rebuilding of Paris in the late 1850s and early 1860s. Nadar
photographed Paris from both above and below ground. Rice's article reproduces and
discusses both his aerial views of the city, shot from aloft in a balloon, and his
subterranean photographs, taken in the tunnels then being excavated for the new
sewerage system.

Music and dance

338 **Opera in Paris, 1800-1850: a lively history.**
Patrick Barbier, translated by Robert Luoma. Portland, Oregon:
Amadeus Press, 1995. 243p.
A translation of *Vie quotidienne à l'Opera au temps de Rossini et de Balzac, Paris,
1800-1850* (Everyday life at the Opera in the era of Rossini and Balzac, Paris, 1800-50),
which provides a history of the Opera de Paris during the Romantic era. This is one of
the few books in English dealing exclusively with the opera in France.

339 **Paris: the musical kaleidoscope, 1870-1925.**
     Elaine Brody. New York: G. Braziller, 1987. 359p. bibliog.
A history of music in Paris from the death of Berlioz (1869) to the 1920s, covering
fifty-five years of creative activity during a time when Paris was seen as the artistic
centre of the world. Brody provides a stimulating discussion of the people, French and
foreign, who met in Parisian musical and artistic circles, pointing out links between
musicians, artists, and writers.

340 **The ballet of the Second Empire.**
     Ivor Guest. London: Pitman; Middletown, Connecticut: Wesleyan
     University Press, 1974. 279p. bibliog.
Although at first glance this study of ballet in the Paris of Napoleon III seems a
somewhat specialized volume, general readers should not be deterred, as they will find
much to interest them. The author's aim is 'to chronicle the events of the ballet and
bring to life some of the people involved in it against the setting of the period . . .
believing that the history of an art form is inseparable from contemporary trends in
thought and the social and political conditions of the time'.

341 **The Ox on the Roof; scenes from the musical life in Paris in the
     twenties.**
     James Harding. New York: St. Martin's Press, 1972. Reprinted, New
     York: Da Capo, 1986. 261p. bibliog.
A study of 'Les Six': composers Georges Auric, Louis Durey, Arthur Honegger,
Darius Milhaud, Francis Poulenc, and Germaine Tailleferre who met at the Boeuf sur
le Toit restaurant in Paris. Harding's book on the group discusses both their music and
their lives from the 1920s to the 1960s.

342 **Listening in Paris: a cultural history.**
     James H. Johnson. Berkeley, California: University of California
     Press, 1995. 384p. (Studies on the History of Society and Culture,
     no. 21).
Johnson has utilized an extensive collection of primary sources to write on an unusual
subject: the history of audience behaviour in Paris from 1750 to 1850, an era when
concert-goers were listening to the music of Rameau, Gluck, Mozart, and Beethoven.
The central conclusion Johnson reaches from his examination of changes in audience
behaviour between the audiences of Rameau and those of Beethoven is that listeners
were gradually silenced. For a study of Parisian theatre audiences see John Lough's
Paris theatre audiences in the seventeenth and eighteenth centuries (London: Oxford
University Press, 1957. Reprinted, 1972. 293p.).

343 **Orpheus in Paris; Offenbach and the Paris of his time.**
     Siegfried Kracauer, translated from the German by Gwenda David,
     Eric Mosbacher. New York: A. A. Knopf, 1938. 373p. bibliog.
     Reprinted, New York: Vienna House, 1972.
Kracauer's work, which has been cited as the best published study of the musical
culture of the bohemian era in Paris, centres around the operettas of Jacques
Offenbach.

344 **The Paris Opera: an encyclopedia of operas, ballets, composers, and performers.**
Serge Pitou.   Westport, Connecticut: Greenwood, 1983-90. 3 vols. in 4.
An alphabetical dictionary of the repertoire and personnel of the Paris Opera from its beginnings in 1671 to 1914 in three volumes: volume one: 'Genesis and glory, 1671-1715'; volume two: 'Rococo and romantic, 1715-181'; and volume three (in two parts): 'Growth and grandeur, 1815-1914'. Entries provide biographical information, plot summaries, and bibliographies.

345 **The art of the Ballets Russes; the Russian seasons in Paris, 1908-1929.**
Militsa Pozharskaya, Tatiana Volodina, foreword by Clement Crisp.
New York: Abbeville Press, 1991. 288p.
A volume consisting largely of illustrations of the costumes and stage sets of the theatrical productions that Sergei Diaghilev's ballet company, commonly known as the Ballets Russes in the West, performed in Paris from 1908 to 1929. The exotic and experimental designs astounded the Parisians of the time and will still delight the reader. Scenery and costumes for the Ballet Russes were designed by such artists as Bakst, Picasso, Cocteau, de Chirico, Braque, and Rouault.

346 **Musicians of to-day.**
Romain Rolland, translated from the French by Mary Blaiklock, with an introduction by Claude Lundi.   New York: H. Holt & Company, 1915. 324p. (The Musicians Bookshelf).
Rolland critiques and compares French and German music of the belle époque. French composers included are Hector Berlioz, Camille Saint-Saens, Vincent d'Indy, and Claude Debussy. The last chapter is 'The awakening: a sketch of the musical movement in Paris since 1870'.

347 **Some musicians of former days.**
Romain Rolland, translated from the French by Mary Blaiklock.   New York: Holt, 1915. 374p.
This book includes a chapter, 'The first opera played in Paris: Luigi Rossi's Orfeo'.

Theatre and film

348 **The Folies Bergères.**
Charles Castle.   New York: Franklin Watts, 1982. 319p. bibliog.
The nude musical spectacle is a special feature of Parisian popular entertainment, and no theatre is better-known for this type of revue than the Folies-Bergères, which inaugurated the vogue at the end of the Second Empire in 1869. Castle's book provides a history of the music-hall and biographical information on those who performed there.

349   **The spirit of Montmartre; cabarets, humor, and the Avant-Garde, 1875-1905.**
       Edited by Phillip Dennis Cate, Mary Shaw.   New Brunswick, New Jersey: Rutgers University Press, 1996. 249p.

A collection of five essays exploring the avant-garde aesthetic in relation to the development of cabaret in Montmartre, focusing particularly on the Chat Noir and the Quat' z' Arts cabarets.

350   **From desire to Godot: pocket theater of postwar Paris.**
       Ruby Cohn.   Berkeley, California: University of California Press, 1987. 204. map.

A study of theatre productions in Paris, from 1944 to 1953. Cohn, who was a student in Paris at the time, states that hers is the only book that 'limits itself to the theater of that decade. . . . [seeking] to recapture performances in their time when the audience [herself included] shivered in the dim intimacy of pocket theaters'. Cohn's first chapter offers a thumbnail sketch of the history of theatre in Paris. Subsequent chapters analyse plays by Pablo Picasso, Jean-Paul Sartre, Antonin Artaud, Jacques Audiberti, Henri Pichette, Boris Vian, Eugene Ionesco, Arthur Adamov, Jean Vauthier, and Samuel Beckett.

351   **The Grand Guignol: theatre of fear and terror.**
       Edited by Mel Gordon.   New York: Amok Press, 1988. 188p. bibliog.

The Theatre du Grand-Guignol, a product of *fin-de-siècle* France, was a feature of Parisian life from 1897 to 1962, providing an arena within which the most sacred taboos surrounding violence and sexuality were outraged. The editor of this book, a professor of drama, traces the history of this lurid form of popular entertainment, discussing its plays, dramatists, actors and actresses, and influence. The book also includes two translations of plays from the Grand Guignol's repertoire: 'The System of Doctor Goudron and Professor Plume', an adaptation by André de Lorde from a story by Edgar Allen Poe; and 'The Laboratory of Hallucinations', by André de Lorde and Henri Bauche.

352   **Paris vu par le cinema.** (Paris as seen through the cinema.)
       Rene Jeanne, Charles Ford.   Paris: Hachette, 1969. 256p.

Although now dated, this remains the only available book-length study of films focusing on Paris. After interesting chapters on the transposition of the Paris of novelists Zola, Balzac, Hugo, Dumas, and Simenon to the screen, the authors discuss the Paris found in the films of French *cinéastes* Louis Feuillade, René Clair, Marcel Carné, Jacques Feyder, Julien Duvivier, Jean Renoir, and Jacques Becker. Other chapters deal with a variety of subjects treated in films about Paris, for example, the representation of the Parisian criminal class, Paris during the Second World War, etc. The final section of the book discusses the Paris that emerged from the film studios of Rome, Berlin, and Hollywood. The filmography, p. 241-46, lists films about Paris through the 1960s. To update this list, readers should consult the filmography compiled by Isabelle Fierro in *Histoire et dictionnaire de Paris* (History and dictionary of Paris) (see item no. 425), p. 1,489.

353   **Nightlife of Paris: the art of Toulouse-Lautrec.**
Patrick O'Connor.   New York: Universe, 1991. 79p.

A selection of Henri de Toulouse-Lautrec's drawings, paintings, and lithographs of
Parisian theatres, cabarets, and brothels. O'Connor comments in his introduction that
'. . . Lautrec's vision [of the celebrated and infamous personalities of nocturnal Paris]
seems like that of a merciless voyeur . . . without sentimentality or censure'.

354   **The Moulin Rouge.**
Jacques Pessis, Jacques Crepineau, English edition edited by Andrew
Lamb.   New York: St. Martin's Press, 1990. 208p.

A profusely illustrated, popular history of the Montmartre night club, the Moulin
Rouge.

355   **Turn-of-the century cabaret: Paris, Barcelona, Berlin, Munich,
Vienna, Cracow, Moscow, St. Petersburg, Zurich.**
Harold B. Segel.   New York: Columbia University Press, 1987. 418p.
bibliog.

Segal begins his detailed account of the cabaret mania that swept Europe in the late
19th and early 20th centuries with a chapter entitled 'Paris: black cats and reed pipes',
p. 1-83, in which he describes and discusses the founding, history, and present fame of
the Chat Noir, the Montmartre cabaret founded by Rodolphe Salis in 1881 which
launched the cabaret movement in Europe.

356   **The Parisian stage; alphabetical indexes of plays and authors
(1800-75).**
Charles Beaumont Wicks.   University, Alabama: University of
Alabama Press, 1950-67. 4 vols. (University of Alabama Studies,
nos. 6, 8, 14).

Provides an alphabetical listing of dramas performed in Parisian theatres from 1800 to
1875. Volume one covers 1800-15; volume two, 1816-30; volume three, 1831-50; and
volume four, 1851-75. The fourth volume contains a 'Cumulative Index of Authors,
1800-1875'.

Fashion

357 The opulent eye: fashions of Worth, Doucet and Pingat.
Elizabeth Ann Coleman. New York: Thames & Hudson/The
Brooklyn Museum, 1989. 208p.

An illustrated catalogue of an exhibition of the fashions of 19th-century Paris
designers Charles Frederick Worth, Jacques Doucet, and Emile Pingat held at the
Brooklyn Museum, New York, from 1 December 1989 to 26 February 1990.

**358 Couture: an illustrated history of the great Paris designers and
their creations.**
Edited by Ruth Lynam. Garden City, New York: Doubleday, 1972.
256p.

A history of the world of Parisian *haute couture*, from its mid-19th-century beginnings
with Englishman Charles Frederick Worth to the 1970s. Separate chapters are devoted
to the top designers: Chanel, Dior, Fath, Courrèges and Ungaro, Cardin, and Saint-
Laurent. The reader is given an inside look at the trade, including a description of the
fashion organization, the Chambre syndicale de la Couture Parisienne. An essay by
model Penelope Portrait depicts the world of the high-fashion mannequin of the
1950s. The book is well illustrated with photographs of the designers and their
creations.

359 Chanel: a woman of her own.
Axel Madsen. New York: H. Holt, 1990. 388p.

A biography of Paris fashion designer Gabrielle (Coco) Chanel (1883-1971), based on
previously published material. Other biographies of Chanel are Edmonde Charles-
Roux's *Chanel: her life, her world, and the woman behind the legend she herself
created* (New York: Knopf, 1975. 380p.), and Amy De La Haye's *Chanel, the
couturière at work* (Woodstock, New York: Overlook Press, 1994. 136p.).

360 **Christian Dior: the man who made the world look new.**
Marie-France Pochna, translated from the French by Joanna Savill, foreword by Stanley Marcus. New York: Arcade, 1996. 314p.

A biography of designer Christian Dior, whose 'New Look' revitalized the postwar Paris fashion industry.

361 **Paris fashion: a cultural history.**
Valerie Steele. New York: Oxford University Press, 1988. 317p. bibliog.

A book 'about the significance and symbolism of fashion in modern society, and an analysis of the reasons why Paris was for so long the international capital of style'. Steele relates fashion to the culture and geography of 19th-century Paris, with a final chapter in which she examines '*Haute couture* in the twentieth century'. The book is based on published sources.

Architecture and Urban Planning

General

362 **La croissance de la banlieue parisienne.** (The growth of the Paris
   suburbs.)
   Jean Bastié.   Paris: Presses Universitaires de France, 1964. 624p.
   maps. bibliog. (Publications de la Faculté des lettres et sciences
   humaines de Paris. Serie 'Recherches' t. 17).
The author's thesis at the University of Paris, this book is an important source for the
history of the urbanization of the Paris Metropolitan area. It includes an extensive and
useful forty-nine-page bibliography.

363 **St. Louis and the court style in Gothic architecture.**
   Robert Branner.   London: A. Zwemmer, 1965. 157p. Reprinted, New
   York: Harper & Row, 1985. (Studies in Architecture, vol. 7).
A study of the architecture of mediaeval Paris during the reign of Louis IX. Branner's
text is enhanced by 140 black-and-white illustrations.

364 **The assassination of Paris.**
   Louis Chevalier, translated from the French by David P. Jordan, with a
   foreword by John Merriman.   Chicago: University of Chicago Press,
   1994. 274p. map.
Chevalier, the pre-eminent historian of Paris, has written an angry book in which he
denounces the destruction of Parisian historic buildings and sites in the name of urban
renewal, particularly the gouging out of Les Halles. The book was originally
published in France in 1977; the English edition has an updated final section:
'Epilogue: Twenty Years Later', p. 260-74, in which Chevalier reviews his earlier
conclusions.

365 **Paris through the ages; an illustrated historical atlas of urbanism and architecture.**
Pierre Couperie, translated from the French by Marilyn Low. New York: G. Braziller, 1971. 1 vol. [unpaged]. maps. bibliog.
This translation of *Paris au fil du temps* (Paris: Editions J. Cuenot, 1968) is a reference work which will be equally useful to students of Parisian history or Parisian architecture. It is a compact atlas that illustrates the growth of the city through a succession of maps on a constant scale, with architectural features indicated – structures which have been destroyed as well as those which still survive. The maps begin with the prehistoric period and end with Paris as it was in 1968.

366 **Paris: a century of change, 1878-1978.**
Normas Evenson. New Haven, Connecticut: Yale University Press, 1979. 382p. bibliog.
A superb, beautifully illustrated case-study of urban renewal and city planning in Paris by an architectural historian.

367 **Cities and people: a social and architectural history.**
Mark Girouard. New Haven, Connecticut: Yale University Press, 1985. 397p. bibliog.
This attractive volume includes two chapters dealing with Paris. In 'Amsterdam and Paris', the architectural history of the city in the mid-17th century is described, and in 'Paris and the boulevards', the urban transfomation that took place in the 19th century is detailed.

368 **Consciousness and the urban experience; studies in the history and theory of capitalist urbanization.**
David Harvey. Baltimore, Maryland: Johns Hopkins University Press, 1985. 293p. bibliog.
A sociological analysis of urban development from a Marxist perspective, centring on Paris in the 19th century. Harvey includes an interesting chapter on Sacré-Coeur, 'Monument and myth: the building of the Basilica of the Sacred Heart', p. 221-49.

369 **Etudes sur les transformations de Paris: et autres écrits sur l'urbanisme.** (Studies on the transformations of Paris and other writings on urbanism.)
Eugène Henard, edited and with an introduction by Jean-Louis Cohen. Paris: L'Equerre, 1982. 364p. maps. (Collection 'Formes Urbaines').
In this book, Jean-Louis Cohen brings together articles by Eugène Henard on town planning for Paris originally published serially between 1903 and 1909. Cohen also provides an introduction to the work of this pioneering city planner. Readers will be struck by the modernity of Henard's vision of a Paris of the future, particularly with regard to his conception of urban transport and the use of metropolitan space for public gardens. For an English-language study of Henard, see *Eugène Henard and the beginning of urbanism in Paris, 1900-1914* by Peter M. Wolf (The Hague: International Federation for Housing and Planning, 1968. 118p.).

370   **Transforming Paris: the life and labors of Baron Haussmann.**
       David P. Jordan.   New York: Free Press, 1995. 455p. maps.
       Jordan assesses Haussmann's drastic mid-19th-century urban renewal of Paris in the
       context of Haussmann's biography.

371   **Histoire de l'urbanisme à Paris.** (The history of city planning in
       Paris.)
       Pierre Lavedan.   Paris: Diffusion Hachette, 1993. 2nd ed. 732p.
       bibliog. (Nouvelle Histoire de Paris).
       An important history of city planning in Paris. This edition is a reprint of the original
       1975 edition with an added 100-page supplement by Jean Bastié bringing the volume
       up-to-date (1974-93) and a new bibliography.

372   **Space and revolution: projects for monuments, squares and public
       buildings in France, 1789-1799.**
       James A. Leith.   Montreal: McGill-Queen's University Press, 1991.
       363p. bibliog.
       A study which includes plans for public buildings in Paris during the Revolution.

373   **Paris nineteenth century; architecture and urbanism.**
       François Loyer, translated from the French by Charles L. Clark.   New
       York: Abbeville, 1988. 478p. maps. bibliog.
       Since 1974, Loyer has directed the Atelier Parisien d'Urbanisme survey of the 19th-
       and 20th-century architecture of Paris. Thus he is well qualified to write this important
       book, which covers a range of subjects relating to the 19th-century reshaping of Paris
       as planned and carried out by the redoubtable Baron Haussmann. Readers will be
       fascinated by his detailed descriptions of building codes, building decoration and
       ornament, and the design of building facades, as well as by the larger topics of
       architecture, and urban planning and renewal. The text is clarified by the ample
       provision of maps and photographs of the city.

374   **De vieux Paris au Paris moderne; Haussmann et ses prédécesseurs.**
       (From old Paris to modern Paris; Haussmann and his predecessors.)
       Andre Morizet.   Paris: Hachette, 1932. 399p. map. bibliog.
       One of the few books on Parisian urban development to cover the architects and city
       planners who succeeded as well as those who preceded Haussmann.

375   **The city as a work of art: London, Paris, Vienna.**
       Donald J. Olsen.   New Haven, Connecticut: Yale University Press,
       1986. 341p. bibliog.
       Olsen links the form and functions of London, Paris, and Vienna to the political
       cultures and social values of their founding societies.

376 **L'oeuvre du Baron Haussmann, Préfet de la Seine (1853-1870).**
(The work of Baron Haussmann, Prefect of the Seine [1853-70].)
Louis Reau [et al.]. Paris: Presses Universitaires de France, 1954.
157p. map. bibliog.

A collection of essays and studies on Haussmann and his reconstruction of Paris that were originally published in the *Revue Urbanisme et Habitation* (July-December 1953).

377 **Haussmann: Paris transformed.**
Howard Saalman. New York: G. Braziller, 1971. 128p. bibliog.
(Planning and Cities).

A succinct study of Baron Haussmann's urban redevelopment of Paris.

378 **The autumn of central Paris; the defeat of town planning, 1850-1970.**
Anthony Sutcliffe. London: Edward Arnold, 1970. 372p. map.

A study of the first to the fourth *arrondissements*, the *centre rive droite*, of Paris, that seeks to explain why the historic centre of Paris has remained virtually unchanged since the mid-19th century despite repeated attempts to modernize it. Sutcliffe considers whether, in the light of the changing functions of the city centre, this survival is a triumph or a defeat.

379 **Paris: an architectural history.**
Anthony Sutcliffe. New Haven, Connecticut: Yale University Press, 1993. 232p.

Lavish illustrations reinforce Sutcliffe's central thesis of the enduring classicism that characterizes the architecture of Paris. Sutcliffe traces the Parisian tradition from Roman times to the emergence of the neo-modernism of the present day, showing how each architectural era contributed to an abiding classical tradition.

380 **Renaissance Paris: architecture and growth, 1475-1600.**
David Thomson. Berkeley, California: University of California Press, 1984. 214p.

An exceptional interdisciplinary study that unites history and architecture to illuminate the transformation of mediaeval episcopal Paris into a renaissance royal capital. Of particular interest in Thomson's book is his account of the building of the Louvre, which he places in the context of the development of luxury residential architecture in Paris.

381 **La Cité renaissante.** (The city reborn.)
Leandre Vaillat. Paris: Larousse, 1918. 102p.

One of the few books that deals with the renovation of Paris in the immediate aftermath of the First World War.

382 **Building Paris; architectural institutions and the transformation of the French capital, 1830-1870.**
David Van Zanten. New York: Cambridge University Press, 1994. 360p. maps.

An important book on the government architectural services that directed urban growth in Paris in the mid-19th century. Van Zanten discusses the replacement of traditional monarchical direction in shaping the city by the emergence of competing architectural bureaucracies. He also contrasts private and institutional building and the contributions to urban entreprise and municipal building made by various architects and administrators.

383 **Designing Paris; the architecture of Duban, Labrouste, Duc, and Vaudoyer.**
David Van Zanten. Cambridge, Massachusetts: MIT Press, 1987. 338p. bibliog.

An authoritative work on important neoclassical and Greek Revival buildings designed by these four architects for Paris in the mid-19th century.

384 **Classical influence on the public architecture of Washington and Paris: a comparison of two capital cities.**
John E. Ziolkowski. New York: P. Lang, 1988. 243p. bibliog. (American University Studies, Series XX, Fine Arts, vol. 4).

Ziolkowski contrasts the neoclassical public buildings of Washington, DC with those of Paris.

An architect's Paris.
See item no. 35.

Architect's guide to Paris.
See item no. 56.

The guide to the architecture of Paris.
See item no. 61.

The Paris of Henri IV: architecture and urbanism.
See item no. 95.

Special features

385 **Paris publicized and privatized: Daniel Buren in the Palais-Royal.**
Dore Ashton. *Arts Magazine*, vol. 61, no. 1 (Sept. 1986), p. 18-20.

Ashton discusses Buren's Project for the Palais Royal, and the politico-artistic controversy generated in France by Buren's proposed transformation of the *cour d'honneur* of the Palais Royal by installing 'graduated, truncated, striped columns and subterranean streams'. The article is illustrated with photographs of the work in progress.

386   **Les travaux souterrains de Paris.** (Underground works in Paris.)
Eugène Belgrand.   Paris: Dunod, 1873-77. 5 vols. and 1 atlas vol.

This massive set is the fundamental work on the Paris water supply. In his first volume, Belgrand provides preliminary material on local sources of the city's water: the Seine; rainfall; and springs and running water. Subsequent volumes cover the way in which water has been brought to the city from the aqueducts constructed by the Romans to the water system of the 19th century. The last volume covers the sewage disposal system of Paris.

387   **The palace of the sun: the Louvre of Louis XIV; with a chapter on materials and structure written in collaboration with Rowland J. Mainstone.**
Robert W. Berger.   University Park, Pennsylvania: Pennsylvania State University Press, 1993. 232p.

A study of classical renovations made to the Louvre during the 17th century.

388   **The French cafe.**
Marie-France Boyer, photographs by Eric Morin, translated from the French by Jacqueline Taylor.   New York: Thames & Hudson, 1994. 112p.

The café is the institution that best epitomizes Parisian social life. In her book, Boyer examines all manifestations of the café: the legendary (e.g. the Deux Magots and Café de Flore), the traditional, the stylish, and the humble.

389   **Private Paris; the most beautiful apartments.**
Marie-France Boyer, photography by Philippe Girardeau.   New York: Abbeville Press, 1994. 192p.

A striking presentation of luxury apartments emphasizing exquisite interior decoration. The work is enhanced by 180 full-colour photographs. Marie-France Boyer is the Paris editor of *The World of Interiors*.

390   **The Louvre; an architectural history.**
Genevieve Bresc-Bautier, photographs by Keiichi Tahara.   New York: Vendome Press, 1995. 224p.

An authoritative illustrated guide to the Louvre's complex architectural history, tracing its transformation through 800 years from fortress to palace to museum. Bresc-Bautier, the Chief Curator of the Department of Sculpture at the Louvre, deftly leads readers through the periods represented in the rooms and halls of the Louvre: the Renaissance Lescot and Lemercier wings; the Baroque Galerie d'Apollon; the classic Colonnade wing; the neoclassical 'Musée des Antiques'; Napoleon III's 'New Louvre'; and the contemporary Pyramid. The volume is splendidly illustrated with over 200 colour plates.

391   **Rough and reddish.**
      Ginger Danto.   *Art News*, vol. 88, no. 5 (May 1989), p. 103-04.
A brief description of the Parc de la Villette, a futuristic 125-acre cultural complex in
northeastern Paris designed by Bernard Tschumi. The park's main attraction is Adrien
Fainsilber's City of Science and Industry, a glass and stainless steel structure that is a
museum of scientific information.

392   **As befits a legend: building a tomb for Napoleon, 1840-1861.**
      Michael Paul Driskel.   Kent, Ohio: Kent State University Press, 1993.
      251p. bibliog.
The author states that until this book, 'no substantial account existed of the process of
building [Napoleon's] tomb in the Church of the Invalides in Paris, or of the problems
and the social meanings that are implicated in it – despite the facts that this is a work
of a major nineteenth-century architect'. The tomb of Napoleon was designed by
Louis Visconti, who also supervised the work of its construction. Driskel's book is a
thorough study of its subject, based on intensive research in unpublished records, and
succeeds in explicating Napoleon's tomb both as a social phenomena and as an artistic
achievement. The book is carefully and sensitively illustrated.

393   **Great hotels of Paris.**
      Bernard Etienne, Marc Gaillard.   New York: Vendome, 1993. 199p.
The highlight of this book is the more than 140 colour photographs of the top-class
hotels of Paris, among them the Ritz, the Grand Hotel, the Louvre Intercontinental,
and the Georges V.

394   **The architecture of death: the transformation of the cemetery in
      eighteenth-century Paris.**
      Richard A. Etlin.   Cambridge, Massachusetts: MIT Press, 1984. 441p.
      bibliog.
A presentation by an architectural historian of the evolution of the design of
sepulchral monuments in Parisian cemeteries during the 18th century. Etlin points out
how changes in funerary architecture mirrored changing attitudes toward life and
death.

395   **The great houses of Paris.**
      Claude Fregnac, Wayne Andrews, preface by Jacques Wilhelm,
      translated from the French by James Emmons.   New York: Vendome,
      1979. 279p.
A superb visual presentation of the architecture and interior decoration of the Parisian
homes of France's most distinguished families.

396   **The statues of Paris: an open air pantheon.**
      June Hargrove.   New York: Vendome Press, 1990. 382p.
Brimming with more than 500 illustrations, 375 in colour, this volume can serve
equally well as a *catalogue raisonné* of the public sculptures admired in the squares
and along the boulevards and streets of Paris, or as a guide for the visitor who seeks a
walking tour of the statues of the city.

397 **Les plaques commémoratives des rues de Paris: étude.** (A study of the commemorative plaques on the streets of Paris.)
Michel Henocq.   Paris: La Documentation Française, 1981. 167p.

A study compiled under the auspices of the Préfecture de Paris of the historical markers that commemorate historical events on the streets of Paris.

398 **Les 200 cimetières du vieux Paris.** (The 200 cemeteries of old Paris.)
Jacques Hillairet (pseud.).   Paris: Les Editions du Minuit, 1958. 428p.

A scholarly study of the places in Paris where the remains of famous people were interred prior to 1860.

399 **The dungeons of old Paris: being the story and romance of the most celebrated prisons of the monarchy and the revolution.**
Tighe Hopkins.   New York; London: G. P. Putnam's Sons, 1897. 265p.

Contains chapters on the Conciergerie, the Dungeon of Vincennes, the Great and Little Chatelet and the Fort-L'Evêque, the Temple, Bicetre, Sainte-Pelagie, the Abbaye, the Luxembourg, the Bastille, and La Roquette. Hopkins has written a romantic account of now-obliterated Paris prisons, organizing his book around anecdotes of famous prisoners.

400 **Gustave Eiffel.**
Henri Loyrette.   New York: Rizzoli, 1985. 223p. bibliog.

The title of the French edition of this book, *Eiffel, un ingénieur et son oeuvre* (Eiffel, an engineer and his work), more aptly describes its contents, for while it is the story of Gustave Eiffel's long life (1832-1923), the author has placed his emphasis on Eiffel's engineering achievements, foremost among which stands Eiffel's masterpiece of iron construction, the Tour Eiffel. Loyrette devotes one-third of his biography of Eiffel to analysing this Paris landmark.

401 **Designing the new landscape.**
Sutherland Lyall, foreword by Sir Geoffrey Jellicoe.   New York: Van Nostrand Reinhold, 1991. 240p.

This book on modern landscaping includes two sections on Paris's Parc de la Villette: 'Parc de la Villette, Paris', by Bernard Tschumi; and 'Bamboo Garden, Parc de la Villette, Paris', by Alexander Chemetoff.

402 **La brique à Paris.** (Brick in Paris.)
Bernard Marrey, Marie-Jeanne Dumont.   Paris: Editions de Pavillon de l'Arsenal; Picard, 1991. 219p. bibliog.

An exhibition catalogue documenting brick buildings in Paris.

403   **Charles Garnier's Paris Opera: architectural empathy and the renaissance of French classicism.**
Christophe Curtis Mead.   New York: Architectural History Foundation; Cambridge, Massachusetts: MIT Press, 1991. 343p.

Built in 1861-75 from the designs of Charles Garnier, the Paris Opera, whose extravagantly embellished facade dominates the Place de l'Opéra, is considered the epitome of Second Empire taste. In his introduction to this book, Mead states that his aim is to explicate the style of this elaborate building by recovering 'the political, economic, institutional, industrial, social, and intellectual circumstances' of the Paris of the Second Empire to which Garnier responded in his design of this monument of French neoclassicism. The book is amply illustrated and provides excellent coverage of such topics as Garnier's life; the Opera competition in which Garnier's design won first place; and the construction of the building.

404   **The studios of Paris: the capital of art in the late nineteenth century.**
John Milner.   New Haven, Connecticut: Yale University Press, 1988. 248p. maps.

In part one of this exceptional study, Milner traces and discusses the art establishments that were institutionalized in 19th-century Paris – the Louvre, the Institut Nationale des Sciences et des Arts, and the Ecole des Beaux-Arts. In part two he focuses directly on the artists' dwellings, both the splendid and the sordid, covering the areas where thousands of Parisian artists lived and worked, from 1879 to 1905.

405   **The Paris Opera: Palais Garnier.**
Jacques Moatti, photographs by Jacques Moatti, texts by Martine Kahane, Thierry Beauvert.   New York: Vendome Press, 1988. 186p.

A translation of *L'opéra de Paris*. A splendidly illustrated work by the Paris Opera's official photographer, this book details the history of the Paris Opera and its impressive building.

406   **L'Etoile.**
Adapted from the French by Christiane Corty Neave.   Paris: Impr. 'le Soleil', 1966. 92p. bibliog.

An attractive presentation of the history of the Arc de Triomphe that stands at the hub of La Place de l'Etoile, which the author describes as a 'wide, sweeping circle of roadway in the heart of Paris, from which twelve great avenues . . . radiate like broad bands of starlight'. The Arc de Triomphe was conceived in 1806, completed in 1836, and has since been a symbol for the French nation and the site of ceremonial events.

407   **Les ponts de Paris.** (The bridges of Paris.)
Renée Plouin, preface by André Chastel.   Paris: Olivier Perrin, 1967. 127p. map. (Collection la Belle Histoire de Paris sur Seine).

A book of black-and-white photographs of Parisian views. The text outlines the history of Paris focusing on the best-known of the city's bridges. Text and photographs are interspersed with quotations from French authors describing Parisian sights.

408 The Palais-Royal, garden of the Revolution.
Catherine Reynolds. *Gourmet*, vol. 49 (April 1989), p. 62 and fol.

A short history of the Palais Royal, built by Cardinal Richelieu in the 17th century, and subsequently the residence of Louis XIV's brother, the Duc d'Orléans. The galleries, shops, and cafés were developed in 1785, the latter becoming a centre for discussions of politically revolutionary ideas.

409 The making of Beaubourg; a building biography of the Centre Pompidou, Paris.
Nathan Silver. Cambridge, Massachusetts: MIT Press, 1994. 206p.

Silver's fascinating narrative brings out all the twists and turns of uncertainty in the conception and building of Paris's main modern cultural centre. It was designed by the then little-known firm of Piano and Rogers, and its architects and builders faced every vicissitude of shifting politics, cultural misunderstanding, and aesthetic criticism in regard to their work before it reached completion in 1977.

410 In the theater of criminal justice: the Palais de Justice in Second Empire Paris.
Katherine Fischer Taylor. Princeton, New Jersey: Princeton University Press, 1993. 161p. (The Princeton Series in Nineteenth-Century Art, Culture, and Society).

A unique type of architectural history. In her book, Taylor emphasizes the role played by decor in the criminal justice system, and the symbolic role of architecture in representing – and often exacerbating – conflicts between judicial and political doctrines and social practice.

411 Notre-Dame of Paris.
Allan Temko. New York: Viking Press, 1955. 341p. map. bibliog.

A lengthy presentation of the history of the design and construction of Paris's cathedral. Temko explores the origins of the idea to build Notre-Dame de Paris and the architectural tradition to which it belongs. The basic plan of the cathedral is given and the various phases of building are elaborated. The book includes plans and photographs, and a chronology of the construction of the church from 1160, when the decision to build was taken, to 1352 and the completion of the screen. Another book on the church is *Notre-Dame de Paris* by Richard Winston, Clara Winston and the editors of the Newsweek Book Division (New York: Newsweek, 1971. 172p.).

Mass Media

412 The first Paris press; an account of the books printed for G. Fichet and J. Heynlin in the Sorbonne, 1470-1472.
Anatole Claudin. London: Printed for the Bibliographical Society at the Chiswick Press, 1898. 100p. (Bibliographical Society, Great Britain. Illustrated Monographs, no. 6).

Claudin recounts the beginning of printing in 15th-century Paris with the press established by the rector of the Université de Paris, Guillaume Fichet. The book includes facsimiles of title-pages of incunabula.

413 Histoire de l'imprimerie en France au XVe et au XVIe siècles.
(History of printing in France during the 15th and the 16th centuries.)
Anatole Claudin. Paris: Impr. Nationale, 1900-15. 5 vols.

The first two volumes of this set were printed especially for the World Fair held in Paris in 1900, and reproduce specimens of incunabula and examples of early Parisian printing. The volumes are also informative on the early history of printing and printers in Paris.

414 The *Paris Herald*: the incredible newspaper.
Al Laney. New York: D. Appleton-Century, 1947. 334p. Reprinted, New York: Greenwood, 1968.

A sprightly, anecdotal account of the Paris *Herald*, from its founding in 1887 to the Second World War.

415 **Histoire des journaux publiés à Paris pendant le siège et sous la Commune: 4 septembre 1870 au 28 mai 1871.** (History of newspapers published in Paris during the Siege and the Commune, 4 September 1870 to 28 May 1871.)
Firmin Maillard.   Amsterdam: Liberach, 1971. 267p.

This work is a reprint of an 1871 publication listing newspapers published in Paris during the 1870-71 Commune.

416 **France and the mass media.**
Edited by Brain Rigby, Nicholas Hewitt.   Houndsmills, England: Macmillan, 1991. 238p. (Warwick Studies in the European Humanities).

A collection of essays discussing the influence of the mass media on French culture in the postwar era.

The Left Bank revisited: selections from the Paris *Tribune* 1917-1934.
See item no. 189.

Newspapers and Periodicals

417 **ICI Paris.**
   Paris: Hachette Filipacchi Publication, 1945- . weekly.
A newspaper-format French-language publication that covers general interest materials pertaining to Paris. It includes film reviews.

418 **L'Officiel des Spectacles: cette semaine.**
   Paris: L'Officiel des Spectacles, 1946- . weekly.
A weekly French-language guide to entertainment in Paris, which lists and reviews films, plays, etc.

419 **Paris le journal.**
   Paris: Association pour l'Information municipale, 1977- . monthly.
This publication for the Parisian municipal government, formerly entitled *Ville de Paris* (City of Paris), provides information for the building and construction industry. Its circulation is around 300,000.

420 **Paris-Sud; organe d'information des arrondissements sud de Paris.**
   Paris: Editions Municipales S.A.R.L., 1961- . monthly.
A general interest publication which focuses on the *arrondissements* in the south of Paris. It incorporates the publication *Vaugirard-Grenelle*.

421 **Une Semaine de Paris-Pariscope.** (This Week in Paris-Pariscope.)
   Paris: Publications Filipacchi, 1923- . weekly.
A French-language guide to films, drama, and other entertainment in Paris that has been published since 1923.

Encyclopaedias, Directories and Reference Works

422 **Dictionnaire de Paris.** (Dictionary of Paris.)
Patrice Boussel [et al.]. Paris: Librairie Larousse, 1964. 591p. maps.
Contains entries on Paris arranged alphabetically from 'Abattoirs' to 'Zoo de Vincennes'. The historical information provided is rich in detail; among the topics covered are 'Clochards' (Tramps), 'Balzac', and 'Crimes célèbres' (Famous crimes). Each *arrondissement* receives an entry, as do well-known buildings. The work also includes well-chosen illustrations and an analytical index.

423 **Dictionnaire des monuments de Paris.** (Dictionary of monuments in Paris.)
Edited by Jean Colson, Marie-Christine Lauroa, introduction by Laure Beaumont-Maillet. Paris: Editions Hervas, 1993. 2nd ed. 917p.
An encyclopaedia of Parisian architecture. The volume is principally arranged alphabetically; information can also be accessed through indexes of architects, painters, and sculptors, and through topographical and subject indexes.

424 **Les armoiries de la ville de Paris: sceaux, emblèmes, couleurs, devises, livrées et cérémonies publiques.** (The armorial bearings of the city of Paris: seals, emblems, colours, mottoes, uniforms, and public ceremonies.)
Anatole de Coëtlogon, reedited and completed by L.-M. Tisserand and the Service historique de la ville de Paris. Paris: Imprimerie nationale, 1874-75. 2 vols. map. (Histoire Générale de Paris; Collection de Documents Publiés sous les Auspices de l'Edilité Parisienne).
A comprehensive and detailed work on the heraldry connected with Paris.

425 **Histoire et dictionnaire de Paris.** (History and dictionary of Paris.)
Alfred Fierro. Paris: Robert Laffont, 1996. 1,580p. maps. bibliog.

A comprehensive reference book on Paris, yesterday and today. The work is divided into five sections, including: a narrative history of the city, prehistory to 1995; a section on the Paris of today, covering administration, society, religion, etc.; a chronology of events in Paris from 40,000 BC to 1995 AD; a dictionary of Parisian topics, from 'abattoir' to 'zone'; and a bibliographical section, which includes the cartography, iconography, filmography, and discography of Paris. The information has been meticulously compiled by the author, the conservateur of the Bibliothèque historique de la Ville de Paris, and can be located through three indexes: people, places, and subjects.

426 **Almanach de Paris; encyclopaedia universalis.**
Michel Fleury, with the assistance of Guy-Michel Leprouax, François Monnier. Paris: Encyclopaedia Universalis France, S.A., 1990. 2 vols. maps.

A chronologically arranged listing of important events in Parisian history, from 53 BC to 1989. Volume one covers dates from Julius Caesar to the end of the *ancien régime*, and volume two from the French Revolution to 1989. The work is profusely illustrated. Appended to volume two are useful lists and illustrations which feature the mayors and archbishops of Paris, the prefects of the Seine and Paris, the prefects of police, and the flags of the sixty Parisian districts.

427 **Dictionnaire historique des rues de Paris.** (Historical dictionary of the streets of Paris.)
Jacques Hillairet (pseud.). Paris: Editions de Minuit, 1987. 9th ed. 2 vols. maps.

The latest edition of the fundamental reference on the history of the streets of Paris, which provides comprehensive, finely detailed street-by-street information. The 9th edition includes the *Supplément au Dictionnaire des rues de Paris* (Supplement to the Dictionary of the streets of Paris) (1972) by Jacques Hillairet and Pascal Payen-Apenzeller. 'Jacques Hillairet' was the pseudonym of Auguste-André Coussillan (1886-1984).

Guide to Balzac's Paris; an analytical subject index.
See item no. 295.

Tout Paris: the source guide to the art of French decoration.
See item no. 333.

The Paris Opera: an encyclopedia of operas, ballets, composers, and performers.
See item no. 344.

The Parisian stage; alphabetical indexes of plays and authors (1800-75).
See item no. 356.

Museums

428 Picasso Museum, Paris.
Marie-Laure Besnard-Bernadac, Michèle Richet, Helène Seckel.   New York: Abrams, 1986-89. 2 vols. bibliog.

The catalogue of the Picasso Museum collection. Volume one covers paintings, papiers collés, picture reliefs, sculptures, and ceramics, and volume two, drawings, water-colours, gouaches, and pastels.

429 The Louvre.
Introduction and commentaries by Michel Laclotte, additional commentaries by Jean-Pierre Cuzin.   New York: Abbeville Press, 1980. 112p. (Abbeville Library of Art).

The nucleus of the Louvre collection was the royal art collection begun in the reign of François I (1515-47), and continued by Henri II, Catherine de Médicis, Louis XIV, and Louis XVI. The royal collection was opened to the public as the Musée de la République in 1793; more paintings were added by Napoleon Bonaparte and Louis XVIII (who contributed the sculpture known as the Venus de Milo). In 1848 the Museum became the property of the state and has since enjoyed state support as well as private bequests. Michel Laclotte is the director of the Department of Paintings at the Louvre.

430 The Musée d'Orsay, Paris.
Introduced by Michel Laclotte, translated from the French by Jane Brenton.   New York: Abrams; London: Thames & Hudson, 1987. 208p.

A catalogue of the collection of the Musée d'Orsay, which has been designated the repository of the state collection of mid- to late 19th- and early 20th-century art. Besides its holdings in painting, sculpture, and decorative and graphic arts, the museum also contains architecture, town-planning, and film collections.

Undiscovered museums of Paris.
See item no. 39.

Knopf guide to the Louvre.
See item no. 48.

Indexes

There follow three separate indexes: authors (personal and corporate); titles; and subjects. Title entries are italicized and refer either to the main titles, or to many of the other works cited in the annotations. The numbers refer to bibliographical entry rather than page number. Individual index entries are arranged in alphabetical sequence.

Index of Authors

Index of Titles

129

Index of Subjects

D

Daguerre, Jacques 335
Daladier, Edouard 191
Dali, Salvador 47, 192
Danton, Georges Jacques 125
Daudet, Alphonse 281
Debussy, Claude 273, 346
Degas, Edgar 323
Delacroix, Eugène 329
Delaunay, Robert 331
Derain, André 327
Deux Magots (café) 388
Diaghilev, Sergei 47, 192, 345
Diaries 161, 185
Dickens, Charles 281, 306
Dictionaries 422-23, 425
  monuments 423
  streets 427
Dior, Christian 360
Directories
  decorative arts and artisans 333
Discography 425
Dogs 62, 148
Doisneau, Robert 14
Dos Passos, John 283
Doucet, Jacques 357
Drama 350-51, 356
Du Maurier, George 281
Duban, Jacques 383
DuBois, W. E. B. 274
Dufy, Raoul 327
Dumas, Alexandre 175, 281, 352
Duncan, Isadora 210, 279
Dungeon of Vincennes 399
Dunham, Katherine 42
Durey, Louis 341
Duvivier, Julien 352

E

Ecole Centrale des Arts et Manufactures 265
Ecole de Physique et de Chimie 217
Ecole des Beaux-Arts 319, 330, 404
Ecole Militaire 135
Ecole Normale Supérieure 263
Ecology 64
Economy 5, 248-50
Edo 98
Education 259-65
  see also individual schools and universities by name
Eiffel, Gustave 400
Eiffel Tower see Tour Eiffel
Ellison, Ralph 42
Elysée 135
Engels, Friedrich 162
Engravings 19
Eugènie, Empress 323
Eurodisney 69
Existentialism, 205, 268
Expatriates 42, 47, 188, 266, 269, 274, 277-79, 282-83, 286-87, 304, 330
Exposition Universelle Internationale (1900) 176, 413

F

Fainsilber, Adrien 391
Fantomas (fictional character) 34
Fashion design 357-58, 361
  see also individual fashion designers by name
Fath, Jacques 358
Faubourg Saint-Germain 295
Faubourg Saint Marcel 106
Faulkner, William 47
Faust, Jessie 274
Favras, Marquis de 130
Ferlinghetti, Lawrence 286
Feuillade, Louis 352
Feyder, Jacques 352
Fichet, Guillaume 412
Film 352
Filmographies 352, 425
Fish 148
Fitzgerald, F. Scott 192, 208, 277, 283, 304
Fitzgerald, Zelda 208, 220
Flâneurs 7
Flaubert, Gustave 275, 284
Folie-Mericourt 241
Folies-Bergères 348
Food and drink 53
  guidebooks 50, 53, 59-60
Ford, Ford Madox 47
Fort-L'Evêque 399
François I 429
Franklin, Benjamin 279, 308
Fulton, Robert 279

G

Gaboriau, Emile 281
Gardens 63, 65, 369, 401
Gare du Nord 253
Garnier, Charles 403, 405
Garvey, Marcus 42
Geography 21
Geology 29, 32
  guidebooks 30-32
  maps 30, 32
Georges V (hotel) 393
Germany 185
Gerôme, Jean-Leon 211, 330
Giacometti, Alberto 327
Gide, André 273
Gilles, Abbot of Saint-Denis 83
Ginsberg, Allen 286
Gluck, Christoph Willibald 342
Goncourt, Edmund de 156
Gould, Anna 279
Grand-Guignol 351
Grand Hotel 393
Great Chatelet 399
Green, Julien 301
Grenelle 71

133

137

Map of Paris

This map shows the *arrondissements* (districts) and *quartiers* (wards) of the city.

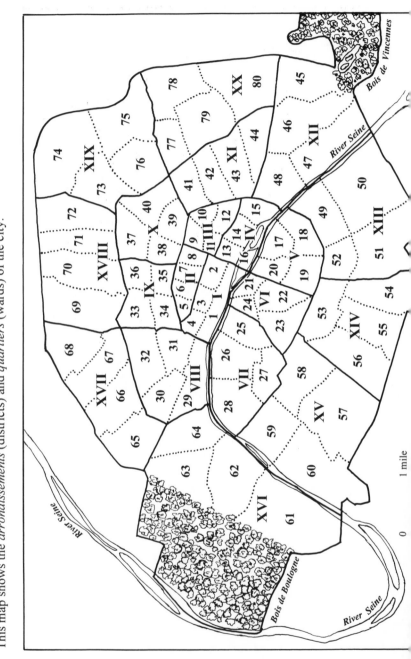

List of *arrondissements* and *quartiers*

I   LOUVRE
1   Saint-Germain-l'Auxerrois
2   Les Halles
3   Palais-Royal
4   Place Vendôme

II   BOURSE
5   Gaillon
6   Vivienne
7   Mail
8   Bonne-Nouvelle

III   TEMPLE
9   Arts-et-Métiers
10   Enfants-Rouges
11   Archives
12   Sainte-Avoye

IV   HÔTEL-DE-VILLE
13   Saint-Merri
14   Saint-Gervais
15   Arsenal
16   Notre-Dame

V   PANTHÉON
17   Saint-Victor
18   Jardin des Plantes
19   Val-de-Grâce
20   Sorbonne

VI   LUXEMBOURG
21   Monnaie
22   Odéon
23   Notre-Dame-des-Champs
24   Saint-Germain-des-Prés

VII   PALAIS-BOURBON
25   Saint-Thomas-d'Aquin
26   Invalides
27   École-Militaire
28   Gros-Caillou

VIII   ÉLYSÉE
29   Champs-Élysées
30   Faubourg du Roule
31   Madeleine
32   Europe

IX   OPÉRA
33   Saint-Georges
34   Chaussée-d'Antin
35   Faubourg Montmartre
36   Rochechouart

X   ENTREPÔT
37   Saint-Vincent-de-Paul
38   Porte-Saint-Denis
39   Porte-Saint-Martin
40   Hôpital Saint-Louis

XI   POPINCOURT
41   Folie-Méricourt
42   Saint-Ambroise
43   Roquette
44   Sainte-Marguerite

XII   REUILLY
45   Bel-Air
46   Picpus
47   Bercy
48   Quinze-Vingts

XIII   GOBELINS
49   Salpêtrière
50   Gare
51   Maison-Blanche
52   Croulebarbe

XIV   OBSERVATOIRE
53   Montparnasse
54   Parc de Montsouris
55   Petit-Montrouge
56   Plaisance

XV   VAUGIRARD
57   Saint-Lambert
58   Necker
59   Grenelle
60   Javel

XVI   PASSY
61   Auteuil
62   La Muette
63   Porte-Dauphine
64   Chaillot

XVII   BATIGNOLLES-MONCEAU
65   Ternes
66   Plaine de Monceau
67   Batignolles
68   Épinettes

XVIII   BUTTE-MONTMARTRE
69   Grandes-Carrières
70   Clignancourt
71   Goutte-d'Or
72   La Chapelle

XIX   BUTTES-CHAUMONT
73   La Villette
74   Pont-de-Flandre
75   Amérique
76   Combat

XX   MENILMONTANT
77   Belleville
78   Saint-Fargeau
79   Père-Lachaise
80   Charonne

ALSO FROM CLIO PRESS

INTERNATIONAL ORGANIZATIONS SERIES

Each volume in the International Organizations Series is either devoted to one specific organization, or to a number of different organizations operating in a particular region, or engaged in a specific field of activity. The scope of the series is wide-ranging and includes intergovernmental organizations, international non-governmental organizations, and national bodies dealing with international issues. The series is aimed mainly at the English-speaker and each volume provides a selective, annotated, critical bibliography of the organization, or organizations, concerned. The bibliographies cover books, articles, pamphlets, directories, databases and theses and, wherever possible, attention is focused on material about the organizations rather than on the organizations' own publications. Notwithstanding this, the most important official publications, and guides to those publications, will be included. The views expressed in individual volumes, however, are not necessarily those of the publishers.

VOLUMES IN THE SERIES

1 *European Communities*, John Paxton

2 *Arab Regional Organizations*, Frank A. Clements

3 *Comecon: The Rise and Fall of an International Socialist Organization*, Jenny Brine

4 *International Monetary Fund*, Anne C. M. Salda

5 *The Commonwealth*, Patricia M. Larby and Harry Hannam

6 *The French Secret Services*, Martyn Cornick and Peter Morris

7 *Organization of African Unity*, Gordon Harris

8 *North Atlantic Treaty Organization*, Phil Williams

9 *World Bank*, Anne C. M. Salda

10 *United Nations System*, Joseph P. Baratta

11 *Organization of American States*, David Sheinin

12 *The British Secret Services*, Philip H. J. Davies

13 *The Israeli Secret Services*, Frank A. Clements